STEP BI STEP

of related interest

Bi the Way
The Bisexual Guide to Life
Lois Shearing
ISBN 978 1 78775 2 900
eISBN 978 1 78775 2 917

It Ain't Over Til the Bisexual Speaks
An Anthology of Bisexual Voices
Vaneet Mehta and Lois Shearing
ISBN 978 1 83997 1 952
eISBN 978 1 83997 1 969

Bisexuality: The Basics
Your Q&A Guide to Coming Out, Dating, Parenting and Beyond
Lewis Oakley
ISBN 978 1 83997 6 445
eISBN 978 1 83997 6 483

Fluid
A Guide for People with Flexible Sexuality
Mark Cusack
ISBN 978 1 80501 3 679
eISBN 978 1 80501 3 686

Trans Teen Survival Guide
Owl and Fox Fisher
ISBN 978 1 78592 3 418
eISBN 978 1 78450 6 629

STEP BI STEP

The Ultimate Guide for Bisexual, Pansexual and Queer Young People

LAURA CLARKE

Illustrated by Laura Tubb

Jessica Kingsley Publishers

London and Philadelphia

First published in Great Britain in 2026 by Jessica Kingsley Publishers
An imprint of John Murray Press

4

Front cover image source: Laura Tubb.

The fonts, layout and overall design of this book have been prepared according to dyslexia-friendly principles. At JKP we aim to make our books' content accessible to as many readers as possible.

A CIP catalogue record for this title is available from the
British Library and the Library of Congress

ISBN 978 1 80501 751 6
eISBN 978 1 80501 752 3

Printed and bound in Great Britain by TJ Books, Padstow, Cornwall

Jessica Kingsley Publishers' policy is to use papers that are natural, renewable and recyclable products and made from wood grown in sustainable forests. The logging and manufacturing processes are expected to conform to the environmental regulations of the country of origin.

Jessica Kingsley Publishers
Carmelite House
50 Victoria Embankment
London EC4Y 0DZ

www.jkp.com

John Murray Press
Part of Hodder & Stoughton Ltd
An Hachette Company

The authorised representative in the EEA is Hachette Ireland,
8 Castlecourt Centre, Dublin 15, D15 XTP3, Ireland (email: info@hbgi.ie)

To everyone who has ever made me feel like
my queerness is something to be celebrated.

And to every young person reading this book.
I hope I can do the same for you.

Contents

Introduction 9

Chapter One: LGBTQIA+ Identities 16

Chapter Two: Bi+ Identities 35

Chapter Three: Myths and Misconceptions 51

Chapter Four: Just a Phase? 73

Chapter Five: Representation 90

Chapter Six: Biphobia 108

Chapter Seven: Intersectional Identities 133

- Bi+ women: Not for you by Laura Clarke 136
- Bi+ men: A vicious cycle by Lewis Oakley 141
- Bi+ trans and non-binary people: Breaking boundaries by Mark Cusack 146

Bi+ people of colour: Bi-passing colonial legacies by AFLO, the poet 151
Bi+ disabled people: Doubly invisible by Eliza Rain 156

Chapter Eight: Coming Out 162

Chapter Nine: Dating 183

Chapter Ten: Sex 201

Epilogue 218

Further Support 221

Acknowledgements 225

Endnotes 227

Introduction

Every bi+ person has their own journey of self-discovery. Here's mine.

When I was 11, I went to a friend's birthday sleepover. I was one of ten giggling girls, hyped up on sugar and the thrill of staying up past our bedtime. Some of them were already my friends, but others I was meeting for the first time, including one particular girl with a long sheet of golden hair, soft skin and a faint aroma of strawberry lip gloss.

I stuck to her like glue, an instant obsession bubbling within me. But I didn't know *why*. Why I wanted her to laugh at my jokes, and no one else's. Why she made me so giddily nervous. Why, when everyone else was watching *Mean Girls*, I was watching her.

When I was 12, at another sleepover, my three best friends danced to Beyoncé, illuminated by the flashes of a music video on MTV. I didn't feel like dancing, instead sat curled up on the cream leather sofa, deep in thought. Watching their hips sway to the beat, something in me solidified. Never one to keep something to myself for more than two seconds, I told my friends to turn off the TV. 'I think...' I said hesitantly, 'I think I might be bisexual.'

If they were shocked, they didn't show it. 'Is this because we were doing sexy dancing?' my friend Rhi asked (her ego as impressive as ever). 'No!' I lied. (Well, a partial lie. Their shaking hips weren't entirely responsible for my bi awakening, but they had certainly helped me realize that I had more than a healthy respect for the female body.) My friends had questions, but their support was undeniable, and we soon went back to dancing – me included.

When I was 13, a friend told me she'd like to kiss a girl, just to try it (yes, the Katy Perry song had recently hit the radio) – 'You're bi, right?' I still wasn't entirely confident that I was, but I nodded. And so my first kiss with a girl happened sitting on my friend's bed, wearing a sleep mask over my eyes because according to her 'it would be weird' if she could see my face. Luckily, I didn't take it as an insult and the kiss itself wasn't half bad.

When I was 14, I was getting changed after PE when another girl accused me of staring at her bra as she took off her top. In reality, my eyes had simply glanced in her direction at the wrong time, but that didn't matter. The laughs and cries of 'lezzer' filled the changing room as my cheeks flushed red. Later that day, I was approached by a younger student I'd never met in the lunch queue – 'Is it true that you're a lesbian?' I glanced around at my sniggering classmates who had obviously put them up to it and said, 'No!' But for some reason, it felt simultaneously like the truth and a lie.

When I was 15, I dated a lot of boys but one in particular made an impact for all the wrong reasons. Our relationship was fleeting in the grand scheme of things, but I spent our time together walking on eggshells, feeling small and ashamed. It was during this specific relationship that I realized for sure that I was bisexual. My tentative 'I think' at 12 had become a confident 'I know' at 15. I told my boyfriend, scared he would be angry, but he didn't seem to care. 'That's fine,' he said. I breathed a sigh of relief and took this as permission to tell the people who didn't already know.

Later that day, I proudly announced my identity to a group of our friends. Everyone was supportive, but my boyfriend looked sullen. When his mood didn't improve, I asked him what was wrong. 'You didn't have to tell everyone,' he grumbled. 'How do you think that makes me look? People will think you're cheating on me with girls.' I remember feeling selfish, and embarrassed, and I quickly promised that I wouldn't tell anyone else.

When I was 16, I went to a house party. While hanging out with a guy and a girl who were in a relationship, somebody (probably me) suggested a three-way kiss. Long story short: too many tongues.

When I was 17, I started crushing on a girl in college. We kissed at parties when we'd had a few drinks, and then acted as if nothing happened the next day. It was the first time I realized I wanted more than to kiss girls – I wanted to date them. I yearned to hold her hand, buy her Christmas presents, and cuddle on the sofa watching TV. She told me, in no uncertain terms, that she was straight. And then another party would roll around, and we'd find ourselves sneaking off to the bathroom to make out. (We've stayed in touch since and, well, she's not straight.)

When I was 18, I went to university to study drama, joined the uni comedy society, and was finally among people who were openly queer. Glorious, loud theatre nerds who were gay, bi and a variety of other flavours of queer that I quickly learned about. For the first time in my life, my bisexuality didn't make me stand out.

When I was 19, I started dating the man who, unbeknown to me at the time, I would eventually marry. When I told him I was bi, he didn't tell me it was embarrassing. And years later, when I told him I was writing a book all about being bi, he told me how proud he was and bought me champagne.

When I was 20, I came out to the only people who didn't

know I was bi – my family. I cried as I told my parents the secret I'd been keeping for the best part of a decade. They had questions. My dad asked, 'How do you know you don't just really *admire* women?' When I asked him the same question in return, he quickly went red and said, 'point taken'. But they were accepting, and that's all I could have asked for.

My mum was confused why 'simply being bisexual' would make me cry and fret so much. To her, it was a huge overreaction to something that wasn't a big deal. She reiterated her love for me in a way that implied I was silly for worrying that anything could change that. I felt hugely fortunate to exist in a family where my sexuality wasn't a big deal, and where, after that initial conversation, everything returned to normal.

These are not my only experiences of discovery and difficulty as a bi person. But they are the moments, peppered throughout my teenage years, that shaped the way I view my bisexuality and, as a result, myself. The emergence of my identity felt clunky, and exciting, and liberating, and scary – often all at the same time. Your own stories may be vastly different to mine. But if you're bi+ (or questioning your identity), it's likely that you relate to at least some parts of my bisexual teenage montage.

When I began to dream up this book, I wanted to create something that would complement your identity, instead of dictating it. I can't tell you how you identify, the exact experiences you will have or the ways in which you should come out. What I can do is share my own stories, my expertise as a sex and relationships educator, and the existing research around bi+ identities to help you navigate your teen and young adult years as a bi+ person.

But I'm only one person, I've only lived one life. So within these pages you will find quotes from a variety of incredible bi+ people – from authors, to activists, to actors and more. These are people I look up to and admire, with a diverse range of identities and experiences, and I hope that you too find inspiration in their success and their stories.

The book also features quotes from bi+ young people themselves, aged 13–19, who are in the midst of navigating young adulthood, just like you! (Some of their names have been changed for privacy.)

Over the course of ten chapters, we'll explore what it means to be bi+, how to handle real-life scenarios like coming out and dating, the key challenges faced by bi+ people, and what we can do to protect ourselves and our community. At the end of each chapter you'll find a 'Step Bi Step' summary of what you've just read, wrapping up the key messages of that section in a few short bullet points.

Some sections might make you feel angry or upset, which is a normal response to reading about discrimination! If this is the case, feel free to take breaks, skip sections completely, or contact one of the services at the back of the book to talk.

Finally, a book can't tell you how you identify. That's something that only you can know. But reading and learning about queerness can help certain puzzle pieces slot into place. When I first heard the word 'bisexual', it felt like an answer to a question I didn't know I'd been asking.

I truly hope that this book helps you on your sexuality journey. But if you turn the final page and realize that you still have things to figure out, or a million more questions to ask yourself – that's completely fine.

My journey to becoming confident in my bisexuality spanned my whole teenage years, and for some people it takes even longer. You don't owe anyone a label, a coming out, or a justification of who you are. You do, however, owe it to yourself to explore all aspects of your identity with self-compassion and gentle curiosity. To never tone down or hide the parts of yourself that feel different, or unconventional, or disruptive. To exist in your entirety, in full saturation.

Chapter One

LGBTQIA+ Identities

If you've picked up this book in particular, then there's a good chance that you're bi+. Perhaps you're already confident in your identity and just want a bit more information, or maybe you're still figuring stuff out and hoping this book will provide you with answers. Either way, I've got you.

I know that you're probably eager to jump straight into the shimmering pool of bi, pan and queer identities. However, first I think it's a good idea to look at bisexuality within the wider context of the LGBTQIA+ umbrella – the alphabet soup, if you like. This step is important for a few reasons:

- First, if you're still in the midst of figuring out your identity, there's always a possibility that bisexual *isn't* your label, and instead you sit somewhere else under the queer umbrella. In this chapter we'll explore the many identities of LGBTQIA+, before venturing into bisexuality in a lot more detail (trust me, a *lot* more detail). This section gives you the opportunity to reflect on other sexual and romantic orientations, like lesbian, gay, asexual and aromantic, so that you have all the information you need to find where you fit in. Think of it as trying on different shirts until you find the one that feels like *you*.

- Maybe you're already one million per cent sure that you're bisexual. Amazing, welcome to the club! But that doesn't make this chapter a complete waste of your time. As a bi+ person, you're now part of a broader community of many queer identities, and it's a good idea to become familiar with the people who will fight by your side for equality. For example, you want asexual people to speak up for bi rights? Then you should also contribute your voice to the fight for ace rights. Be a good neighbour and learn all you can about your queer pals!
- Many people hold multiple identities under the LGBTQIA+ umbrella. Bi+ is a sexual and/or romantic orientation, but what about your gender identity? Or sex assigned at birth? These are areas you hopefully want to learn more about so you can piece together the full jigsaw puzzle that is you.

Now, before we break down the LGBTQIA+ acronym and what all of those letters mean individually, let's talk about some of the main aspects of gender and sexuality more broadly. Namely – sex assigned at birth, gender identity, gender expression, sexual orientation and romantic orientation.

Sex assigned at birth

Your body is made up of many, many parts. Some parts you can see because they're on the outside of your body, and some you can't because they're on the inside.

There are certain parts of our anatomy that everybody has – brain, lungs, liver, nose, mouth, to name a few. But some body parts are only held by (roughly) 50% of the population, and the other (nearly) 50% have different parts. These are called your sex characteristics and they're responsible for why you're labelled male or female at birth (or intersex – we'll get on to this soon!). We're often told that our 'sex' is down to whether we have a penis or a vagina, but it's not quite that simple. So, let's explore our sex characteristics in a little more detail.

Genitals

Your genitals are the reproductive organs that you have between your legs. People are typically considered male when they have a penis, and usually considered female if they have a vulva and a vagina.

Quick anatomy lesson: a vulva refers to the external parts of female genitalia, such as the labia (lips) and the clitoris. Lots of people incorrectly call the vulva a 'vagina' but the vagina is actually on the inside – it's the hole where period blood comes from, or from where a baby might be born. Another common misconception is that urine (pee) comes out of the vagina. It doesn't – it comes from the urethra, which is a separate hole entirely. That's why you're able to pee with a tampon in!

Gonads

Your gonads are the organs responsible for producing reproductive cells. People who have a penis typically also have testes (balls) which hang outside their body under the penis, and produce sperm. And people who have a vagina usually have ovaries inside their body which produce eggs.

Chromosomes

Chromosomes are tiny little structures inside our body that make up who we are (our DNA). Chromosomes come in pairs and most people have 23 sets. Twenty-two of these pairs of chromosomes are called autosomes and are found in bodies with penises *and* bodies with vaginas, but the 23rd set are called sex chromosomes and will typically differ depending on the genitals you have. Usually, if you have a penis, you will have XY chromosomes, and if you have a vagina you'll likely have XX chromosomes.

Hormones

Hormones are chemicals that tell your body what to do. While there are lots of hormones that we all share, there are also some key differences between the sexes, especially when it comes to steroid hormones.

Steroid hormones are produced by your gonads (your testes or ovaries) and are responsible for the way your body changes during puberty. Two of these hormones are testosterone and oestrogen. Despite what you might have been told, testosterone and oestrogen are found in both male and female bodies. However, male bodies typically have higher levels of testosterone than female bodies, and female bodies have higher levels of oestrogen than male bodies.

Secondary sex characteristics

Your secondary sex characteristics come into play during puberty when your hormones begin to tell your body that it's time to grow up. In male bodies, the secondary sex characteristics usually include the voice deepening, shoulders broadening and facial hair growing. For female bodies, typically the hips will widen, breasts will grow and periods will start. There are some changes that are shared by male and female bodies, such as the growth of pubic hair, and getting taller.

Typically, somebody who has a penis will also have testes, XY chromosomes, higher levels of testosterone, more facial hair and a deeper voice. And usually, somebody who has a vagina will also have ovaries, XX chromosomes, higher levels of oestrogen, breasts and wider hips.

Notice how I keep saying 'typically' and 'usually' when I talk about sex characteristics? This is because some people are intersex, which is something we'll explore in more depth later in the chapter...

Gender identity

Okay, so if sex assigned at birth is all about the physical components of your body and your anatomy, then what's gender identity? Some people use the terms 'sex' and 'gender' interchangeably, but in recent years many people have begun to differentiate between the two.

Put simply, your gender is who you are on the inside, and is not defined by your physical body parts. Our society splits people into two categories – men and women –

depending on the anatomy they have, and then expects them to look, sound and act a certain way, purely because of that anatomy. This is called the gender binary and it's kind of designed to divide men and women, rather than celebrate our similarities. If you've ever heard someone say that 'pink is for girls' or 'boys shouldn't cry' then you've already witnessed the gender binary in all of its suffocating glory. Sex educator Emily Nagoski describes how gender is assigned to us at birth and the impact this can have on us as we get older:

> On the day you were born – or maybe even earlier – some adult looked at your genitals and declared, 'It's a boy!' or 'It's a girl!' or 'It's an intersex child!' Along with that declaration comes a cultural 'handbook' – a package of rules and regulations about how to live in this body, what kinds of toys you should play with, what kinds of people you should love, what kinds of feelings you're allowed to express and what kinds of feelings you will be punished for expressing, and lots of other obligations about what goes into being a 'boy' or a 'girl'.[1]

It's worth noting that the gender binary is something humans pretty much invented. We know this because gender norms change throughout time, and differ between cultures. Did you know that in Victorian England, pink was considered to be a boy's colour and blue was considered feminine? Or that numerous cultures around the world have more than two genders, such as the Bugis people of

South Sulawesi, Indonesia, who recognize five different gender identities?

For lots of people, their gender identity and their sex assigned at birth match or feel similar. If you were assigned male at birth, and you feel like a boy/man, or assigned female at birth and feel like a girl/woman, then you might describe yourself as cisgender. Cis- is a Latin prefix which basically means 'on the same side'. So your gender is 'on the same side' as your sex.

But for some people, their gender identity does not align, or fit comfortably, with the sex they were assigned at birth, and these people may consider themselves to be transgender. Trans- is also a Latin prefix meaning 'across from' or 'beyond'. We'll explore trans identities in more detail later in the chapter.

Gender expression

Your gender identity is who you are. But your gender expression is all about how you *express* who you are and present yourself to the world. Gender expression includes things like clothes, hairstyle, makeup, name, pronouns, how you walk, how you talk, and so on.

Many people use gender expression to show the world how they identify on the inside. For example, a woman might opt for fashion choices which are considered stereotypically feminine, such as skirts or long hair. But some people like to dress in a way that society doesn't see as aligning with their gender identity or sex. There are plenty of women who hate dresses and only wear trousers, and lots of men who wear their hair long and flowing.

Some people purposefully dress in a way that doesn't match their gender identity, because to express their true self would be dangerous, or would 'out' them to other people. People who are trans, but not yet out, might wear clothes or express themselves in a way that aligns with the sex they were assigned at birth, even if this doesn't reflect who they really are.

Sometimes people wear certain types of clothing to reflect who they are on the inside, but other times, it's simply because they think it looks cool. Think about people who wear band t-shirts. Some people are huge Guns N' Roses fans, and wear merch to express their love of the band. Other people just think the t-shirts look cool, and couldn't name a single Guns N' Roses song. If you can't always tell if someone is a Guns N' Roses fan from their shirt, then you can't always know someone's gender identity from their gender expression.

And some people simply don't care about their gender expression. They don't necessarily feel the need to express themselves through the way they dress, and simply want to throw on something comfy and get through the day. To them, clothes are just things you wear to keep you warm (and because if you didn't, you'd pretty quickly be arrested!).

Gender expression is really important to some people, and less important to others. But what is always important is that we never assume someone's identity from the way they appear. The only way you can truly know someone's gender is if they tell you.

Sexual and romantic orientation

Your sexual and romantic orientation are about who you are attracted to. (There is a difference between the two, which we cover in lots of detail in the next chapter.)

Some people are attracted to people of only one gender; others are attracted to multiple genders. Lots of people don't experience attraction to other people at all. All are normal, all are fabulous. Research shows us that most people are heterosexual (straight) – this means that they are women attracted to only men, or men attracted to only women. But while heterosexual may be the most common orientation, it certainly isn't the only one!

The alphabet soup

Now that we have an understanding of sex, gender and sexuality, we can begin to explore how these components can present in different people and make up queer identities. We've already touched upon some identities that sit outside of the LGBTQIA+ umbrella – cisgender and heterosexual (people who are both are sometimes referred to as cishet). But what do all of those different letters stand for?

Lesbian

Lesbians are women (cis or trans) who are attracted to other women. Some non-binary people also use this term, and some people define lesbianism as 'non-men who are attracted to non-men'.

Gay

The word 'gay' can refer to men (cis or trans) who are attracted to other men, but this label is also frequently used as an umbrella term to refer to anybody who isn't straight. Some queer women prefer the term 'gay' to 'lesbian' and some people like to use 'gay' alongside other terms, such as 'bi' or 'pan', to express that they are attracted to people of the same gender as themselves.

Bi

Okay, you probably know this one! And if you don't, you sure will by the end of this book. People who are bi are attracted to people of more than one gender. Bi+ is an umbrella term, and people under the bi+ umbrella may use a variety of terms to describe themselves.

Bi+ is the term you'll see me use the majority of the time throughout this book, because it recognizes that not everyone who experiences attraction to multiple genders (multi-gender attraction) uses the label 'bisexual' or 'bi'. We'll cover this, and plenty more about bi+ identities, in Chapter Two.

Trans

Trans people are folks whose gender does not match, or does not sit comfortably with, the sex they were assigned at birth. They may have been told they were a boy or a girl when they were young, but as they grew up, this didn't feel like an accurate description of them as a person.

Trans is an umbrella term, encompassing many different identities, including identities that sit outside the gender binary. People who are non-binary, genderfluid, genderqueer, agender (and many more identities) experience their gender somewhere in between, or outside of, the gender binary.

There are lots of things that trans people may do to feel comfortable in their gender. Some trans people might want to alter their bodies by taking hormones or having surgery, but some trans people will not. Taking hormones or having surgery may be affirming to some trans people, but it doesn't make somebody 'more' trans – being trans is about who you are, and not how your body looks.

Some people get confused between gender identity and sexual orientation when it comes to trans and non-binary people. They think that because somebody is one letter in the LGBTQIA+ acronym, that they can't also be another. But this isn't true! There are transgender and non-binary people of all orientations – straight, gay, lesbian, queer, bi+, asexual, you name it. Gender and orientation are different things and therefore don't come as a package deal.

> *My family always assumed I was a lesbian, because of the way I dressed, and how I felt about females I'd met. I came out as trans to most of my family first – then saying I was bisexual/omnisexual was easier.*
>
> (WILL (HE/HIM), AGE 16)

Queer

Queer is an umbrella term that encompasses all non-cishet identities. Some people use queer to describe their sexuality, while others use queer to describe their gender, or sometimes even other aspects of themselves that don't conform to societal norms. Many people may describe themselves as queer in addition to other labels (for example, I personally use both 'bisexual' and 'queer').

> I've just always fancied everyone, of all genders. The label came gradually. I now embrace 'queer' because it also encompasses my fatness, non-binary-ness and neurodivergence. (SOFIE HAGEN (SHE/HER), COMEDIAN AND AUTHOR OF *HAPPY FAT* AND *WILL I EVER HAVE SEX AGAIN?*)

Queer is a word with a complex history. In the past, it has been widely used as a slur against LGBTQIA+ people. Because of this, some people today don't like the term. As a good rule of thumb, only call somebody queer if you know for sure that they use that word to describe themselves.

Intersex

Intersex is unique because it isn't a sexual orientation or a gender identity – it's all to do with anatomy. Cast your mind back to earlier in the chapter when we discussed sex characteristics and how we all have different sex-specific traits that make up our bodies. Well, people who are intersex have one or more sex characteristics that don't meet the typical notions of either a male or female body.

There are lots of different ways that somebody could be intersex – variations in genitals or gonads, in hormones or chromosomes. Sometimes doctors can tell that a baby is intersex when they're born, because their genitals may look a little different. But lots of people don't realize they're intersex until later in life, because there are no visual differences on the outside of their body.

Being intersex is more common than you might think – around 2% of the world's population are intersex (it's as common as having red hair!). Fun fact: The word to describe somebody who is not intersex is 'endosex'.

Asexual

People who are asexual (or 'ace' for short) feel little to no sexual attraction towards other people, and might not have much interest in having sexual partners. Most asexual people choose to abstain from sex altogether, because they find the thought of it unappealing. On the other hand, some ace people *do* engage in sexual activity for a variety of reasons. Every ace person is different and will have their own feelings about sex.

A quick note: If you're a young person, it's possible that

you might not have experienced the desire to have sex yet. I remember learning about sex when I was a child and finding the thought of it disgusting! But as I got older, and went through puberty, I began to develop sexual feelings towards others and the idea of sex slowly became something I was interested in. The same might happen for you. But if, in time, the feelings of sexual attraction don't show up, you might find that asexuality best describes your experience. The only way to know is to wait and see!

Aromantic

Aromantic ('aro') people experience little-to-no romantic attraction towards other people and may not be interested in having romantic relationships. If you're confused about the difference between sexual and romantic attraction, we cover this further in Chapter Two. Some people are both aromantic and asexual; however, lots of people experience sexual attraction but no romantic attraction, or vice versa.

+

Finally, the plus at the end of LGBTQIA+ represents all the other wonderful, vibrant non-cishet identities that aren't listed in the acronym. For example, pansexual or non-binary – these identities may fall under the umbrellas of 'bi' or 'trans' respectively, but could also be included in the 'plus'. It's impossible to list every queer identity (this book would never end!), so the plus is a great way to recognize that these identities are still included and welcomed within our community.

At this point, you might be asking why non-straight people are grouped together with those who are intersex, or people who have trans identities. If all of these things are so different, what binds us together? Well, in some way, we all defy the gender binary and its incredibly strict rules about what your body should look like, how you should act, and who you should love. Being a bisexual trans man is very different from being a cis lesbian woman – but both have broken out of the boxes they were placed in when they were assigned female at birth. Both have broken society's 'rules' of how to behave as a 'female' person.

As Shon Faye writes in *The Transgender Issue*: 'Homophobia and transphobia share much of the same DNA. To the patriarchy, we all do gender wrong.'[2]

LGBTQIA+ people are unique and face different barriers depending on identity and background, but in so many ways we are fighting the same fight – to be our full, marvellous, colourful selves.

> *My favourite thing about being queer is breaking away from patriarchal, heteronormative expectations of who we should be! Whether that's setting our own beauty standard, expressing ourselves through style, or building community on our terms, the way*

> *we reject what's expected of us and embrace who we really are is beautiful.* (MEGAN JAYNE CRABBE (SHE/HER), CONTENT CREATOR, AUTHOR AND PRESENTER)

And now that we've finished our trip down the rainbow road of queerness, let's venture further into the whole point of this book – bi+ identities.

Step Bi Step...

- As a queer person, it's important to have an understanding of LGBTQIA+ identities that are different from your own. This not only helps you to better define your own identity, but makes you a better ally to your queer siblings. We need to look after one another.

- Sex assigned at birth, gender identity, gender expression, sexual attraction and romantic attraction are all different. Some parts of ourselves are determined by our anatomy, and others are more about who we are on the inside, or who we find attractive.

- You can't guess somebody's identity from the way they look – only if they tell you!

- Queerness is vast and there are hundreds, if not thousands, of LGBTQIA+ identities – some are about gender, some are about attraction and some are about anatomy. What we have in common is that we are the minority in a world where most people are cisgender, heterosexual and endosex. As a result, we experience similar (but not identical) types of oppression. The best way to fight this oppression is together.

Chapter Two

Bi+ Identities

It's finally time to dive head first into the world of bi, pan and queer identities! As mentioned in Chapter One, bi+ is an umbrella term used to describe a variety of identities in which someone feels attraction towards people of more than one gender (also known as multi-gender attraction).

Modern descriptions of bisexuality often refer to it as attraction to more than one gender, or to attraction to your own gender and others. You may encounter older definitions of bisexuality which define it as attraction to 'both men and women', but as our understanding of gender has evolved to recognize non-binary and genderqueer people, so have definitions of being bi.

A popular definition of bisexuality, and my personal favourite, comes from bi+ activist Robyn Ochs:

I call myself bisexual because I acknowledge that I have in myself the potential to be attracted – romantically and/or sexually – to people of more than one sex and/or gender, not necessarily at the same time, not necessarily in the same way, and not necessarily to the same degree.[1]

I love this quote because it bursts bisexuality wide open, recognizing it as an umbrella term, and a spectrum. It says that no two bi+ people are exactly the same, and that a person's relationship with their own bisexuality can evolve over time. While labels alone may seem like a corner we're backing ourselves into, broad and inclusive definitions like this feel more like venturing into a vast and expansive maze, a labyrinth of different possibilities and discoveries.

If I had to give my younger self advice, I'd tell him that labels shouldn't be limiting; they should be empowering. I was so fixated on whether I was straight, gay, bi or something else, that I couldn't actually enjoy any sexual experiences for a long time.

> *Relax. Breathe. Discovering your identity is a journey. You'll get there in time.* (ZACHARY ZANE (HE/HIM), COLUMNIST AND AUTHOR)

Bisexual is only one multi-gender attracted identity, so throughout this book I'll mostly be using the term bi+ to refer to anyone who experiences attraction to more than one gender. This includes people who are bisexual, pansexual, polysexual, omnisexual, queer and other multi-gender attracted people who don't identify with any of these labels.

While each of these identities has its own nuances and differences, they also have a lot in common, as they are all non-monosexual identities. While 'monosexual' refers to people who only experience attraction to people of one gender, such as heterosexual or homosexual people, 'non-monosexual' people instead experience attraction to more than one gender.

Non-monosexual people, regardless of their specific label, will probably share certain life experiences – including similar types of oppression and discrimination (more on this in Chapter Six). As such, this book addresses bi+ identities as a whole, but also recognizes that the individual identities within this community are not identical, and that a preference for a particular label should always be respected.

Which label is *my* label?

You might already know which label(s) you identify with – if so, that's great! But if not, and you're looking for more information, this section can act as a guide to help you to find a word that accurately reflects your multi-gender attraction.

Remember, this guide is just that – a guide! The identities within this chapter are not the only non-monosexual identities that exist, just some of the more common ones. Their descriptions are also deliberately simplistic and may not capture the full breadth of these identities. You don't need to tick every box in a column to 'qualify' for that label and your own personal definitions of these labels might differ – that's okay! You're also free to disregard this guide entirely if you want to – there are no hard and fast rules.

Some people (like me) find labels comforting – a way of better understanding themselves and their community – while others feel that they are restrictive. You may choose not to label your identity at all, or you might decide that you want to use multiple labels to capture your identity in full – either way, it's 100% your choice.

'Bisexual' might be your label if...

- You experience attraction to more than one gender.
- You want a label that is better understood, and doesn't require *as much* explanation when you come out.

- You like 'bi' as an umbrella term, even if you identify with aspects of other multisexual identities.
- You simply connect to the word 'bisexual', or to the colours of the bisexual flag (pink, purple and blue).

'Pansexual' might be your label if...

- You experience attraction to people of all genders or experience attraction regardless of gender.
- You feel 'gender-blind', meaning that gender identity or gender expression doesn't factor into why you're attracted to somebody (for example, you're not necessarily attracted to masculinity, femininity or androgyny, just the person underneath).
- You simply connect to the word 'pansexual', or to the colours of the pansexual flag (pink, yellow and blue).

'Polysexual' might be your label if...

- You experience attraction to multiple genders, but not all genders (i.e. you may be attracted to men and non-binary people, but not women).
- You may have a preference for one gender over others, or experience stronger attraction towards a certain gender.
- You simply connect to the word 'polysexual', or to the colours of the polysexual flag (pink, green and blue).

'Omnisexual' might be your label if...

- You experience attraction to all genders, but you're not 'gender-blind' (i.e. gender or gender expression *does* factor into your attraction to somebody).
- You are attracted to different genders in different ways.
- You simply connect to the word 'omnisexual', or to the colours of the omnisexual flag (different shades of pink, blue and purple).

'Queer' might be your label if...

- You experience attraction to more than one gender.
- You would like a deliberately vague term to describe your multi-gender attracted identity, or you're still in the process of deciding which label is right for you and 'queer' works as an accurate, but non-specific, placeholder.
- You are also trans or non-binary and would like a term that fully captures your non-heterosexual, non-cisgender identity.
- You simply connect to the word 'queer', or to the colours of the queer flag (black, blue, green, white, yellow, red and pink).

For some people, all it will take is reading a definition of an identity label to know that it describes them – something will just *click*. But others will need more time to mull things over or experiment with using different terms before finding the right fit. Your identity isn't any less valid if you sometimes feel unsure, or if it took a while to figure out. Identifying yourself and coming out as non-monosexual is a big deal for a lot of people, so it's natural to want to take your time before pinning your label to your chest for all to see, either metaphorically or with a snazzy Pride flag pin.

> I started realizing I was bisexual at the start of high school. I found people attractive no matter the gender and then, with the rise in social media, I was able to put two and two together and realize that it was okay to feel this way. However, I currently identify as queer –that's just a preference of labels, I still feel the same sexuality-wise. (RIOT (XE/XEM/THEY/THEM), AGE 19)

Same same, but different

While I've tried my best to identify the distinctions between each non-monosexual label, it is worth noting that there is *a lot* of overlap between these identities and, to some people, the minor differences between these labels won't matter. If this describes you, and you're sat here thinking 'why not keep it simple and stick with "bisexual"?' then you are more than welcome to use the label 'bisexual' for yourself.

While the distinction might not matter to you, the important thing is that it *does* matter to some people. And those people deserve to have their chosen label respected and upheld. If you have a preference for the term 'bisexual', then it makes sense that other people may have a preference for a different label.

Additionally, you might be reading this thinking, 'Wait, I've been calling myself "pansexual" but the description of "polysexual" is more accurate. Do I need to change my label?!' To that I say: not if you don't want to! Everyone's relationship with their label is personal, and no one has a right to tell you that you're wrong in how you define yourself. However, if you do decide to change how you describe your sexuality, that's also completely valid – it's never too late to switch up labels.

> There's no rush. You don't have to have an answer. Some people never 'figure it out'. Labels are rough tools rather than boxes. Take what feels useful and don't worry about the rest. (LOIS SHEARING (THEY/SHE/HE), AUTHOR OF *BI THE WAY*, CO-EDITOR OF *IT AIN'T OVER TIL THE BISEXUAL SPEAKS* AND FOUNDER OF THE BI SURVIVORS NETWORK)

When I realized I was attracted to multiple genders, 'bi' was the only term I knew that accurately described my feelings, so I clung to it. It wasn't until my late teens and early twenties that I discovered different labels, like 'pansexual' or 'omnisexual'. I often wonder, if I was a teenager today, would I gravitate towards 'bi', knowing how many other options I have? Of course, I could very easily adopt a new label if I wanted to, but by this point I've called myself 'bi' for so long that it just feels so *me*.

Similarly, I have friends who feel a stronger connection to a certain multisexual label, but instead use 'bisexual' for ease. Most people have a basic understanding of what bisexuality is, but perhaps haven't heard of lesser-known terms. Telling somebody you're omnisexual may open you up to even more questions that you don't necessarily want to answer every time you share your identity with someone.

As you can see, there are many different reasons as to why somebody might choose one label over another. Only you get to choose how you define your sexuality – after all, you know you best!

Sexual vs. romantic attraction

But what does it mean if you feel different types of attraction towards different genders? What if guys, gals and non-binary pals turn you on, but when you picture your wedding, you can only really imagine marrying a woman? Or perhaps you're open to a relationship with someone of any gender, but it's only men who appear in your sexual fantasies?

This, my friends, is called the Split Attraction Model.

The Split Attraction Model is the idea that a person's sexual and romantic attraction can exist separately from one another. What this means in practice is that somebody might not be sexually and romantically attracted to the same genders – the two do not always overlap.

Let's break down some of the differences between sexual and romantic attraction.

You might be sexually attracted to someone if...

- Thinking about them, being around them or being touched by them makes you feel turned on. Your body might feel tingly or sensitive and you might experience warmth, throbbing or aching in your genitals that feels kind of nice. If you have a penis, you might get an erection (your penis getting hard) and if you have a vulva, you might feel your vulva begin to self-lubricate (get wet).
- You enjoy imagining them touching you in intimate places on your body (such as your chest, or your genitals) or you like to imagine touching them in intimate places on their body. This is called fantasizing and some people do this while masturbating (touching their body – usually their genitals – for the purpose of sexual pleasure).

- You would like to see them naked, or you would like them to see you naked.
- You would like to have sex with them, or think you might like to have sex with them at some point in the future.

It's normal and healthy to find yourself developing sexual thoughts towards people during your teen years (and also normal if you do not!). However, it's important to remember that most countries have something called an age of consent, which is the age that you are legally allowed to engage in sex or sexual activity. In the UK, the age of consent is 16 and in the USA it varies between 16 and 18, depending on state. We'll talk more about consent in Chapter Ten, which is all about sex.

For now, just remember that just because you're having sexual thoughts about somebody, it doesn't necessarily mean that you're ready to act upon these thoughts.

So how does romantic attraction differ?

You might be romantically attracted to someone if...

- You like spending time with them and want to form a close bond with them that goes beyond friendship.
- You can't stop thinking about them and maybe feel a little obsessed with them.

- You want them to be your 'special person', and you theirs.
- You want to spend a lot of one-on-one time with them, perhaps going on dates or entering into situations that are typically considered 'romantic'.
- You want to be physical with them in a non-sexual way. For example, cuddling, kissing, holding hands, wrapping your arm around them or playing with their hair.
- You daydream about a future with this person, perhaps living together, getting married or raising a family.

Once again, sexual and romantic attraction are experienced differently by every individual so these bullet points only act as a guide.

If you believed everything you saw in TV shows, movies and books, then it would be easy to think that everyone experiences romantic and sexual attraction towards the same people, that *all* relationships have the sexy stuff *and* the lovey-dovey stuff. But, in the real world, that's not always the case.

There are a huge variety of ways that multi-gender sexual attraction (multisexual) and multi-gender romantic attraction (multiromantic) can manifest. The grid here contains nine potential possibilities for you to explore:

		I'm romantically attracted to...		
		People of one gender	**People of multiple genders**	**Nobody**
I'm sexually attracted to...	**People of one gender**	You might be monosexual and monoromantic (e.g. straight, gay or lesbian)	You might be monosexual and multiromantic (e.g. heterosexual and biromantic)	You might be monosexual and aromantic (e.g. aromantic lesbian)
	People of multiple genders	You might be multisexual and monoromantic (e.g. pansexual and homoromantic)	You might be multisexual and multiromantic (e.g. bi, pan, etc.)	You might be multisexual and aromantic (e.g. aromantic and omnisexual)
	Nobody	You might be asexual and monoromantic (e.g. asexual and heteroromantic)	You might be asexual and multiromantic (e.g. asexual and biromantic)	You might be asexual and aromantic. (i.e. aro ace)

When a person's sexual and romantic attraction align, they may just use one word to describe themselves rather than two. For example, somebody who is pansexual and panromantic might simply use 'pansexual' or 'pan' as a shorthand for their full multi-gender attracted identity.

Bi and ace, bi and aro

At this point, you may realize that you can simultaneously be bi *and* asexual, or bi *and* aromantic. The difference is that bi asexuals might feel *romantic* attraction towards more than one gender (but little-to-no sexual attraction), while bi aromantics may feel *sexual* attraction towards people of multiple genders (but little-to-no romantic attraction).

If you're a bi ace or a bi aro person, you might find that you question your identity more than other bi folks, or even wonder if you're a part of the bi community at all. I'm here to assure you that no matter how your attraction manifests itself, you are 100% bi enough and you belong!

I'm still confused!

As we conclude this chapter, I want you to check in with yourself. If you feel affirmed in your identity, or that some of your questions have been answered – great! But if you're thinking, 'This all just seems so *complicated!*' then I want you to breathe. Take a second and remind yourself that you don't owe anybody a thorough, in-depth explanation of your identity. This isn't a test that you're going to fail, or a competition to see who knows themselves best.

If you want your bi identity to be simple, it can be. Because it's yours. And if it feels confusing or messy or as if it doesn't fit neatly into a box, that's amazing. Because queerness is *all about* not forcing ourselves into boxes that don't feel comfortable. Within this chapter, I've presented a few different ways that being bi+ can manifest, but the truth is there are as many different, unique ways to be bi+ as there are bi+ people. And (you'll get sick of me saying this) every identity is valid, but even more than that, every identity is beautiful.

> You are not just 'valid'. You are magnificent. You are wonderful. You are a blessing. Your existence in the world makes it better. You don't just deserve to be 'accepted'. You deserve to be celebrated for all the beautiful things that you are, and all that you make possible just by existing. You deserve happiness. You deserve love. You deserve to thrive. You deserve everything good in the world.
>
> (SHIRI EISNER (SHE/THEY), ACTIVIST, WRITER AND AUTHOR OF *BI: NOTES FOR A BISEXUAL REVOLUTION*)

Step Bi Step...

- No two bi+ people are exactly alike, and bisexuality itself can be fluid over the course of somebody's life.

- There are lots of different bi+ identities, including (but not limited to) bisexual, pansexual, omnisexual, polysexual and queer. The definitions of these identities have a lot of overlap and some bi+ people use labels interchangeably, but the distinctions are important to other people. Everyone's label should be respected.

- You do not have to choose a label at all if you don't want to, and a label doesn't need to be a 100% perfect fit for you to use it. It's your choice!

- Some people experience romantic attraction and sexual attraction to different genders. Some bi+ people don't experience sexual attraction (biromantic asexuals) and some bi+ people don't feel romantic attraction (bisexual aromantics). If this is you, you are still a part of the bi community and you are welcome!

- If you don't fit neatly into an identity label, or you're still figuring yourself out – that's okay. It's not a race, or a competition. You're you, and you're amazing.

Chapter Three

Myths and Misconceptions

The world has a lot (and I mean *a lot*) of opinions about bi+ people, and many of them aren't exactly glowing endorsements.

LGBTQIA+ identities have become a hot topic in recent years and this boom in discussion has pushed many of us to challenge the harmful views and stereotypes we hold – but learning is a process. Some allies-in-progress still believe biphobic myths because they don't know otherwise, but when presented with new information, they welcome the opportunity to learn. Nobody grows without making mistakes.

However, some people just don't want to learn. Bisexuality disrupts their worldview – one where monosexuality is superior, or the only valid option. Perhaps, when these people make harmful claims about bisexuality, it doesn't come from a place of misunderstanding or ignorance, but from anger or fear that things are changing.

The intent may be different, but the result is the same – negative stereotypes about bi+ people continue to make their way into the world. Maybe you've heard some of these stereotypes before – from friends or family, or in the media. Maybe you've wondered if they were true, and doubted your own identity. Or maybe you've known deep down that they're wrong, but struggled to articulate why.

Sometimes, these negative thoughts can come from within. Perhaps you've found yourself trying to disprove your own bisexuality, using common bi+ myths as your core argument. 'Your honour, I simply cannot be bisexual because [insert bi+ misconception here].' This is called internalized biphobia – it's when we use stereotypes about bisexuality to deny our identity, or to shame ourselves for who we are.

When it feels as if the whole world is telling you that your identity isn't real, or that you're a bad person, it can be easy to start believing it yourself. But here's the thing – they're wrong and, in this chapter, we'll find out why. We'll explore some of the most common misconceptions about bi+ identities and behaviours, taking it one myth at a time, to try and figure out if there's any truth to these claims.

As you work your way through this chapter, I encourage

you to keep an open mind. To feel happy and confident in your bisexuality, you may need to challenge outdated or harmful beliefs that you hold. This can be hard, but it's the key to becoming a more compassionate person – not only to others, but to yourself.

Ready? Let's jump in.

'Bisexuality isn't real, it's called "being confused"!' – MYTH

There are many things that confuse me in life (I'll be honest and say that I still can't do long multiplication in my late twenties) but my bisexuality is not one of them. I, along with hundreds of thousands of other bi+ people, am confident in my identity. And you can be too, even if you're not quite there yet.

But don't just take it from me. Bisexuality dates back over 2500 years, with bisexual behaviours recorded in

Ancient Greece, Rome, Japan and China.[1] When the word 'bisexual' was first coined in the 1800s, it initially referred to individuals with both male and female sex characteristics – people we would call intersex today. It was first used to describe a sexual orientation towards more than one gender in the early 20th century.[2]

But despite its evidence throughout history, bisexuality is still viewed with cynicism by many – bisexuals are frequently labelled as 'confused' and 'undecided' (even though over 2500 years of bi-ness would make for *a lot* of confused people!). The denial of bisexuality, or the failure to acknowledge it, is called 'bi erasure' and it's something we'll go into more detail about in Chapters Five and Six.

But ultimately, we don't need research to know that we exist. I know I am bi in the same way I know that I have a heart – I feel it within me, constant and strong. And even if you don't have the same unwavering certainty as I do – even if you're in the process of questioning who you are – know that you are still the biggest expert on yourself. Nobody has the power to tell you that what you're feeling isn't real.

'Bisexuality is rare' – MYTH

Bisexuality is not only real, it's *common*. Studies have shown that bisexuals make up a slight majority of people who don't identify as straight – in the USA, for example, bisexuals account for 57% of LGBTQ+ adults.[3] Such high numbers of bisexuals within the LGBTQIA+ community, combined with their erasure, has earned bi+ people the nickname of the 'invisible majority'.

But what's more, the number of people who identify as bi is increasing. In 2022, 1.5% of people in the UK aged 16+ reported that they were bisexual. This is almost double the amount of people in 2017 (0.8%).[4] While 1.5% might still feel like a small number, it amounts to over 600,000 people in the UK alone, and doesn't even include...

- bi+ young people aged under 16
- those who didn't feel comfortable disclosing their genuine sexual orientation
- non-monosexual people who don't identify with the label 'bisexual'. In addition to the 1.5% of people who identified as bisexual, 0.6% selected 'other', which could include other non-monosexual identities such as pansexual or queer.[5]

It's also really important to note that the increasing rates of recorded bi+ people doesn't necessarily mean that there are more bi+ people now than there were in 2017 – there are just more people who feel comfortable enough to share their identity with researchers. As society becomes more open-minded towards non-straight identities, queer people feel more free to be their true selves.

And what's more, even if bi+ identities were super rare, that wouldn't take away from their worth. We don't claim that rare animal species are undeserving of our attention – we care for them, learn as much as we can about them and discover how they make our world a more beautiful and interesting place. So, why should we treat LGBTQIA+ identities any differently?

'Bisexuality is a transphobic identity. It implies that there are only two genders!' – MYTH

While historically, 'bisexuality' has been defined as attraction to 'both men and women' or 'people of both genders', as our understanding of gender has evolved, the definition of bisexuality has evolved too. We now recognize that not everybody fits into the categories of 'boy/man' and 'girl/woman' (hey there, non-binary readers!).

This shift in our perception of bisexuality and gender came earlier than you probably assume. In 1990, a bisexual magazine called *Anything That Moves* published its 'Bisexual Manifesto', declaring bisexuality to be a fluid identity:

> Do not assume that bisexuality is binary or duogamous in nature: that we have 'two' sides or that we must be involved simultaneously with both genders to be fulfilled human beings. In fact, don't assume that there are only two genders.[6]

In the years since, many definitions of bisexuality have been updated to reflect our current understanding of gender. The Cambridge Dictionary defines bisexuality as 'the state of being attracted to people of your own gender and people of a different gender'[7] and Stonewall's online glossary describes being bi as 'a romantic and/or sexual orientation towards more than one gender'.[8]

'But wait, doesn't bi literally mean two?!' Great question – I'm glad you asked! Yes, in many contexts it does – for example, a bicycle is a vehicle with two wheels; 'biannual' means to happen twice a year. But language is funny, and there's often an exception to the rule. 'Bilingual' refers to somebody who speaks two languages, but the Linguistic Society of America states that it can also be used to refer to those who speak *more* than two languages.[9] In this instance, and in the case of 'bisexual', 'bi' is used to mean *at least* two.

There are also several other words that don't quite do what they say on the tin. Bi activist Marcus Morgan makes a great point: 'If you hear "Bisexual Visibility Day is September 23rd" and don't angrily complain sept- means seven, then maybe shut up about bi- means two.'[10]

So no, the term bisexuality does not exclude non-binary identities. Words mean what we use them to mean – they do not define themselves. As our understanding of bisexuality expands and evolves, so too does the word.

In a way, I've always known I was bi. The word has always felt like home in some way, although when growing up I was ashamed that it felt like home. Even into my late 20s, I felt like the word 'bisexual' couldn't be the right one because 'bi' meant 'two', and I didn't want to identify with anything that invalidated anyone's gender identity.

It took me a while to realize that bisexuality has always been about disrupting binary systems. Like everything else, we've taken that prefix 'bi' and made it our own, and now we have a glorious gender-inclusive word to call our home. (JEN WINSTON (SHE/THEY), AUTHOR OF *GREEDY: NOTES FROM A BISEXUAL WHO WANTS TOO MUCH*)

'You're only bi+ if you're equally attracted to men and women' – MYTH

This myth is all too common, but it sort of falls apart once you debunk the myth that bisexuality excludes non-binary identities (as we discussed in the previous section). Bisexuality cannot be defined as an equal attraction to men and women if it extends *beyond* attraction to men and women.

So wait, does that mean bisexuality is one-third attraction to men, one-third attraction to women and one-third attraction to people of different genders? Or maybe it's a

50/50 split between masculine traits and feminine traits, regardless of gender identity?

Well, in reality, everyone is different. No two bi+ people are going to experience attraction in exactly the same way. The following graphs all represent bisexuality!

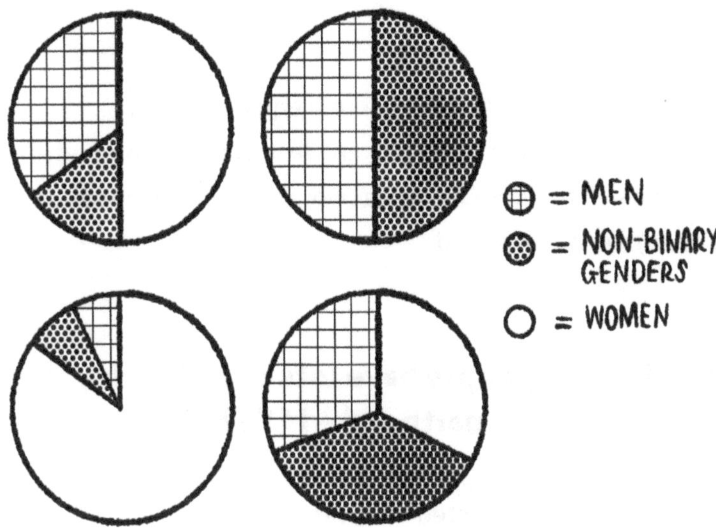

These charts only account for a tiny, tiny number of the ways in which somebody may be bisexual. Bisexuality is an expansive identity, and looks different for everyone.

Additionally, bisexuality can evolve and change over the course of a lifetime. For some, this might be a gradual shift – maybe in their twenties, they find themselves mostly attracted to people of the same gender and over time, their attraction to people of other genders deepens. But for others, it can vary based on the month, week, day or even hour!

Personally, there are times in my life where I find myself exclusively attracted to people with more feminine traits for a few weeks, and then suddenly something shifts and I'm all about masculinity. Then, a short while after that, androgyny is really up my street!

If you don't experience completely equal levels of attraction, it doesn't make you any less bi than somebody who does. In the Bi+ Olympics (wow, that totally needs to happen), we *all* take gold.

'All bisexual people have lots of sex with lots of different partners' – MYTH

Somebody being attracted to a wider range of people doesn't necessarily mean that they have more sexual partners than anyone else.

Now, some bi+ people absolutely do have sex with lots of people. But so do many other people, of all sexualities! And on the other hand, lots of bi+ people don't engage in casual sex and instead prefer to date or sleep with one person at a time.

This stereotype of bisexuals having lots of casual sex is

almost always meant as a criticism – they may be saying 'bisexuals sleep with lots of people' but what they're really saying is 'bisexuals sleep with lots of people *and that's bad*'.

This is textbook slut-shaming. Slut-shaming is when people – often women, girls and LGBTQIA+ people – are judged, mocked or looked down on for having (or being assumed to have) lots of sex. Some people wrongly believe that those who have sex with lots of partners are worth less than those who have sex with just a small number of people. Please join me in formally declaring this belief to be gross.

It is *your* decision who you share your body with. Some bisexuals have sex with hundreds of people, some bi+ people only do it with one or two, and some never have sex at all! Whichever path you decide to follow, you are always worthy of respect and a life free from prejudice and mistreatment. To learn more about how to have sex safely, check out Chapter Ten.

'Bi+ people will never be content in a monogamous relationship because they're greedy' – MYTH

Monogamy is the practice of having a relationship with one person at a time. Despite the pervasive misconception that bi+ people aren't satisfied unless they're having sex with people of all genders, many, many bisexuals (myself included) have and enjoy successful monogamous relationships.

Even in a monogamous relationship, there are many ways to explore your bisexuality. Some people still have fun crushing on celebrities of different genders (as I write this, my lock screen is a really hot pic of Taylor Swift...). And lots of bi+ people enjoy exploring their sexuality during masturbation – whether this is using your imagination to fantasize about a variety of different people, or looking at pictures or videos that depict people of multiple genders.

Taking a step away from sexual attraction, you might also continue to immerse yourself in bi+ culture – this could be reading books or watching TV shows where the characters reflect your own identity or experiences, or going to Pride events or bi+ meetups where you can socialize with other bi, pan and queer people. Check out some tips on how to honour your bi+ identity in a monogamous relationship in Chapter Nine.

There are so many ways to feel fulfilled in your bi+ identity while in a monogamous relationship. That being said, monogamy *doesn't* work for everyone, and polyamory (the practice of being in romantic relationships with multiple people at the same time) is also a dynamic enjoyed by many bi+ people. Polyamory is different to cheating, because everybody involved is aware and has given consent. We'll talk more about polyamory in Chapter Nine too.

Don't try to force yourself into a relationship style that doesn't suit your needs, just because society has told you that it's the thing we should all be striving for. Happily-ever-afters aren't one-size-fits-all.

'Bisexual people are always unfaithful' – MYTH

A 1997 study of straight people's attitudes towards bisexuals found that bi people were perceived as more likely to cheat on their partners than heterosexuals.[11] This mistrust extends to monosexual gay and lesbian people, some of whom refuse to date bi+ people, out of fear that they will inevitably cheat on them.

Now, the purpose of this book isn't to argue that all bi+ people are angelic and flawlessly moral. We're humans. So yes, plenty of bi+ people are unfaithful. But that doesn't mean that the identity itself is the driving force behind cheating. Bi+ people cheat because *people* cheat.

Being bi+ is one trait that a person may have. The ability or desire to cheat is another. The two are not linked and the idea that they are is incredibly harmful to bi+ individuals. This myth once again stems from the stereotype that bisexuality is inherently greedy, wanting more than your share, or that bisexuals are sex-obsessed, morally corrupt people.

Your trust in a person should never be determined by

their sexuality, only by how trustworthy they have proven themselves to be.

'Bisexuals are more likely to have STIs' – IT'S COMPLICATED

STI stands for sexually transmitted infection – an infection that can be passed on through sexual contact with other people. An extension of the myth that bi+ people have lots of sexual partners is that, as a result, bisexuals are more likely to carry and pass on STIs.

Historically, bi+ people have experienced high levels of stigma surrounding STI transmission, particularly in relation to the AIDS crisis in the 1980s. When HIV (the infection that can develop into AIDS) was first discovered, it was incorrectly believed to be a disease that solely affected gay men. But over time, more and more straight people began to become unwell with the disease.

From this, the conclusion was drawn that bisexuals were the bridge – passing HIV from the gay community to the straight community.[12] While it's true that some transmissions may have occurred this way, we now know that HIV can also be transmitted through other (non-sexual) means, such as in blood or breast milk.

Okay, but is it true that bi+ people are more likely to have

STIs? Well, yes. But it's really more complicated than that. Research has shown that bisexual people are more likely to test positive for STIs and, in some cases, less likely to get tested in the first place.[13]

However, this doesn't necessarily mean that bi+ people are having more casual sex than monosexual people (which is often our assumption when we think about STI transmission). In fact, there are several potential reasons for higher STI rates among bisexuals, including limited access to contraception, avoiding healthcare services and testing due to fear of discrimination (we'll take a deeper dive into what this discrimination looks like in Chapter Six) and a lack of appropriate sex education.

Sometimes people ask me why I became a sex educator – this is why. Comprehensive, accessible and queer-inclusive sex and relationships education is essential – it allows people of all genders and sexualities to gain autonomy over their bodies and their health.

'Bisexual boys are really just gay, and bisexual girls are actually straight' – MYTH

Hmm, isn't it funny how in both of these scenarios, it's assumed that who we're *really* attracted to is a man? How interesting...

Many believe that phallocentrism (a word I stumble over pronouncing every time I say it) is partly to blame for this myth. Phallocentrism is defined by the Cambridge Dictionary as 'the fact of having the male, or male sexual feelings or activity, as the main subject of interest'.[14] Basically, it's a fancy way of saying that men (and penises) are the most important in our society and, as a result, make the most desirable partner.

The belief that women are inferior and men are superior is called misogyny. And this myth is misogynistic as hell. Not only is it a phallocentric view of the world, it is also sometimes used to humiliate bi+ people by forcing them into positions that are seen as less powerful or degrading.

We sadly live in a world where (some) people believe that it's embarrassing or humiliating to be a man who has sex with men. There is a societal idea of what is 'manly', and being gay isn't it. Obviously, this is nonsense, but it does mean that bi+ boys and men are assumed to *actually* be gay instead of bi, but too embarrassed to admit it.

Additionally, same-gender sexual activity between women is seen as existing for the enjoyment and pleasure of boys and men. The result of this is the belief that bi+ girls are really just straight, and only hooking up with other girls to appear more sexy to the men they *actually* want to sleep with. (Can I scream now please?!)

> *I was brought up to think that some women would kiss each other for male attention, probably because of 'I Kissed a Girl' by Katy Perry. Even though there were situations where I was alone with a woman, with no man to impress, and I would want to kiss them anyway, it still didn't click for me. I still thought I was doing it to be attention-seeking.* (LEANNE YAU (SHE/THEY), POLYAMORY EDUCATOR AND INFLUENCER)

Do I even need to tell you that this myth is all kinds of false and harmful? Just to be absolutely clear – bi+ people are real and valid. Men aren't the most important beings to ever walk the earth. And only *you* get to define your sexual orientation. (Honestly, three amazing sentences to repeat in the mirror on the days you're having a sexuality crisis. You're welcome.)

'Once you're in a relationship, you're no longer bisexual' – MYTH

'Wait, so by saying you're bisexual you're admitting that you're attracted to other people besides your partner?!' Yes, yes I am.

Can we *please* abandon the idea that once we're in a relationship we all cease to feel attraction towards other people? It is normal and healthy to find other people cute when you're in a monogamous relationship. It isn't cheating and it doesn't mean that you love your partner any less. If anything, isn't it a higher compliment to your partner that you're attracted to other people but you *choose* to be with them every day because they're just so special to you?

Let me put it this way. Imagine you go shopping, and you're looking for something to wear to a party on Saturday night. You search and search and eventually you find the *perfect* pair of jeans. You try them on, they fit like a dream, and you buy them.

As you walk down the street, completely happy with your purchase, do all the clothes in other shop windows suddenly look hideous to you? Did your ability to appreciate other clothes vanish the second you handed over your cash? Probably not. It's likely that, as you walk to catch your bus, you still take a few moments to window shop. It doesn't mean you're intending on buying anything else and it doesn't mean that you're any less happy with the jeans in your bag.

Identity and attraction are completely different from behaviour. You can be bi+ and attracted to people of multiple genders but only date a person (or people) of one gender. Your bisexuality doesn't disappear in a puff of smoke the minute you go on a date, or kiss someone, or get married. In fact, the #StillBisexual movement is dedicated, in part, to highlighting the voices of bi+ people who are in long-term relationships and are – you guessed it – still bisexual.[15]

In 2022, I got married. As a testament to my identity, I attached a bi flag pin to my bouquet, symbolizing that I wasn't leaving my bisexuality at the altar that day – I was carrying it into my marriage with me. And as I walked down the aisle with the cool metal of the pin brushing against my fingers, I knew two things: that I was about to commit myself to the man I love more than anything, and that I was still, undeniably and fabulously, bisexual.

'Bisexuals are "less queer" than other LGBTQIA+ people' – MYTH

This feeling is common among bi+ people, and is often heightened for those in 'straight-presenting' relationships (for example, a bi woman dating a man or a bi man dating a woman). Bi erasure, combined with the notion that we lose our bisexuality once we enter a relationship, can make us feel like our queerness is less valid than our monosexual gay and lesbian peers. I've felt this, and I know so many other bi+ people who have too.

You may find yourself wanting to 'prove' your queerness through the people you date, and the way you present yourself, but why? Where does a desire to be 'queer enough' (whatever that means) come from?

> There's no wrong way to be queer. You don't have to look a certain way or 'wear the uniform'. Queerness should not be just another box you have to fit into. Queerness is freedom. There are no rules. Love whoever you want, wear whatever you want, live however you want.
>
> It's so easy to go from struggling to fit into the 'straight' role for years and then realize you're queer, only to think, 'Well, now do I have to wear Doc Martens and have short hair forever? Why don't I love Chappell Roan's music, like all the other queer people?' I get the need and the importance of the 'queer uniform' – I celebrate it and love it. It's just not me. I needed someone to tell me that I'm queer enough, regardless of how I look or how I live my life. I might still need to be told that. (SOFIE HAGEN (SHE/HER), COMEDIAN AND AUTHOR OF *HAPPY FAT* AND *WILL I EVER HAVE SEX AGAIN?*)

It's normal to want to feel that you are part of a community. For so long, queer people have been made to feel unwelcome by heterosexual, cisgender people. It can feel as if a door has been closed on us. So when we see another door, open wide, leading to a warm room adorned with Pride flags and filled with people rocking blue hair and dungarees, our gut instinct is to run towards it as fast as we can. To come in from the cold.

And when, to our shock, we're also turned away from our new-found safe haven, it can hurt ten times as hard.

But take it from me, you do belong in that room. Your current relationship, your dating history and the clothes you wear don't matter. You're bi, and that means you're queer enough. You get lifetime access. And any queers who say differently simply aren't worth your time. So, come on in.

'Bisexuality is just a phase' – IT'S COMPLICATED

You know what? I'd love to go into this one in more detail, and we will, in the next chapter...

Step Bi Step...

- There are a multitude of myths and misconceptions about bi+ people. Some are simply not true, and others are slightly more complicated.

- Often these myths come from a place of ignorance – a lack of education around bi+ identities. But sometimes people perpetuate these myths to intentionally cause harm, or because bisexuality disrupts their worldview.

- One of the main reasons that bi+ myths are so damaging is that bi+ people are so different from one another. We can't possibly all be categorized into one short statement.

- Some bi+ people *do* fit the stereotypes of bisexuality – many of us date multiple people, have lots of casual sex and feel confused about our identities – and that's totally fine! Combating stereotypes or myths isn't about denying these parts of ourselves, or brushing them off because we find them shameful. It's about reiterating that bi+ people are as complex, rich and diverse as anyone else.

Chapter Four

Just a Phase?

'It's just a phase, you'll grow out of it!'

'You'll pick a side eventually.'

'Everyone thinks they're bi at one point or another.'

If you've been at the receiving end of any of these phrases – usually accompanied by a smug, knowing smirk – you're not alone. The sentiment that 'bisexuality is just a phase' goes back a long way and doesn't show many signs of letting up any time soon.

Sigmund Freud, a famous Austrian neurologist, plays a large role in this pervasive idea. Freud believed that all humans are born bisexual but, once grown up, eventually identify as heterosexual (straight) or homosexual (gay). This theory was popularized in the early 1900s, so being straight was seen as the ideal outcome. And while homosexuality was definitely frowned on, it was still considered to be preferable to bisexuality.

Freud's theory painted bisexual adults as 'immature' and 'infantile'. In a 2009 paper on bisexuality, clinical psychologist Esther Rapoport explains Freud's theory using the following metaphor:

> To use a culinary analogy, heterosexuality, in this view, may be likened to a cake that tastes just right and homosexuality, to one prematurely taken out of the oven; bisexuality, to continue with the analogy, is not a cake at all but amorphous dough whose future edibility is as yet undetermined.[1]

This attitude, of bisexuals as immature or underdeveloped, still lingers today. We're seen as fence-sitters, confused, or keeping our options open. And sadly, teenagers and young people bear the brunt of this belief.

As a pre-teen, I remember learning about my impending adolescence through a variety of sources – school, parents, friends, books. There was a lot of talk about periods, and getting sweatier, and fancying people. I especially remember being told that it was normal for teenagers to find themselves attracted to people of the same sex. But (and here was the caveat) these feelings were simply the result of RAGING HORMONES and would probably go away. Imagine my surprise when same-gender attraction rocked up and very much stuck around.

I did, however, know several people for whom those feelings *did* go away – friends who went through a brief 'am I queer?' period. They'd confide in me (the token bisexual) that they thought they fancied a girl, but the feelings left as quickly as they came and many of them have grown into confidently heterosexual women. Some realized that they actually wanted to *be* the cool girl they liked, rather than be *with* her (the classic 'girl crush'). Others genuinely held sexual or romantic feelings, but they went away and didn't come back for a member of the same gender again.

It's very possible that you yourself have already done a lot of deliberating over your sexuality. Maybe you have the same questions swirling around in your brain as I did as a teenager – what if I'm straight and it's just my crazy hormones? Or maybe I'm gay but I've been conditioned by society to find the opposite sex attractive? Will I feel the same way when I've finished puberty? What if I come out as bi and then my feelings change? How can I be sure about my sexuality when I haven't even had sex yet?!

Don't worry. We're about to explore these two specific outcomes in a lot more detail – the possibility that your bisexuality *is* a phase (and why that's okay!), and the possibility that it's not.

'It's just a phase!'

I was 15 when Lady Gaga dropped the queer anthem 'Born This Way'. The song is a testament to being who you are – in its lyrics, Gaga namechecks gay, lesbian, bi and trans identities specifically, celebrating and affirming queerness with the argument that, you guessed it, we're born this way.

Now, listen – I've danced to 'Born This Way' at many a Pride party. But while I love the song, it does raise some complicated questions about the rigidity of our sexuality. Gaga certainly wasn't the first person to claim that LGBT people are 'born this way' – an argument that has historically been used by lesbian, gay and bi+ people to push back against people trying to 'turn us straight'. It says, 'I didn't choose this identity, I was just born this way.'

The first issue with this narrative is that it makes us almost apologetic in our queerness. That our non-heterosexual or non-cisgender identity is in some way a flaw that needs to be justified. That it's only acceptable if we 'can't help it'. Now, being queer isn't a choice, but if it was, why would it be a bad one? As bi+ activist Lois Shearing says in an article for *Cosmopolitan* – 'If bisexuality was a choice, I'd choose it any day.'[2]

But there's another key issue with the 'born this way' argument, and it's the one I'd like to explore in more detail. While you may have heard cries of 'we were born this way' from Pride parades, or in online LGBT spaces, it's likely that you've also heard that sexuality is fluid from the very same people. Which feels kind of...contradictory.

Bi+ people are already disadvantaged by the 'born this way' narrative, due to the common misunderstanding that we can simply date somebody of a different gender, effectively choosing a 'heterosexual lifestyle'. Because we have the ability to be attracted to people of another gender, and gay and lesbian people don't, our identities aren't validated by the same 'I just can't help it!' argument. Now, this is obviously rubbish – we don't have control over who we find attractive or fall in love with. If we did, I could have avoided a lot of heartbreak from straight girls in my teen years.

What's more, plenty of bi+ people simply don't feel that their sexual orientation is something they were born with, and that will remain a constant throughout their whole lives. Their attraction to different genders ebbs and flows over the months, years and decades and, yes, goes through phases!

But here's the thing – phases are valid. Going through a phase, whether that's related to a hobby, liking a certain band, or even your sexuality or gender, doesn't mean that it wasn't authentic for you at the time. Imagine you played guitar for ten years and then eventually fell out of love with that particular instrument and took up the piano instead. Nobody would say, 'Oh, so you weren't *really* a guitar player, it was just a phase.' Two things can be true – you were a guitar player *and* it was a phase! Lots of people are genuinely attracted to more than one gender, sometimes for years, and then something changes. And that's okay.

> As a child, I was only really aware of girls around me, despite being assigned female at birth. As I slowly discovered I was transgender, this somehow shifted into solely attraction to men. Over the years, it's been a fluid and gradual discovery that has taken a lot of difficulty to understand. Even now, being queer, specific labels like bisexual and pansexual feel tricky.
> (WREN (HE/HIM), AGE 17)

One common biphobic stereotype is that bisexuality is just a stepping stone to someone realizing they're 'fully gay'. This sentiment is harmful and reductive because it just isn't true for a vast number of bi and pan people. But it would also be harmful to disregard the people for whom this is their exact experience.

Sometimes we go through phases where, in hindsight, we recognize that we weren't being authentic to our true selves. As a teenager, I went to a lot of concerts. I convinced myself that I loved them – the music, the crowds, the hype – because deep down I was terrified of being left out of an experience that all of my friends loved. It was only once I got older that I came to terms with the fact that I'd been lying to myself and that concerts really aren't for me – I hate standing in one spot for hours with sore feet, smushed up against other people, with nowhere to put my drink, and feeling sweaty and overstimulated. But for years I told myself I loved something I didn't, just to fit in.

Some people *do* come out as bi before realizing they are actually gay, possibly because compulsory heterosexuality – the theory that everyone is assumed and expected to be straight – means we find it hard to imagine a world in which we don't experience attraction to the opposite sex. And while this isn't the experience for a lot of bi+ people, and shouldn't be assumed to be, it doesn't mean this journey isn't okay.

> Enjoy the uncertainties and ambiguities of your sexuality. When I was young I so wanted my sexuality to be simple, easy to explain and easy to find community around. I spent a lot of time scrutinizing my attractions in my own head, rather than enjoying them. I could see that straight people and gay people had communities around the fact that their sexualities seemed simpler to explain to people. But a community that comes at the expense of being easy to explain isn't really a community, and it doesn't feel better than being lonely. Like many other things in a bi life, things were better when I realized I shouldn't have to choose. (TANAKA MHISHI (HE/HIM), AUTHOR OF *SONS AND OTHERS: ON LOVING MALE SURVIVORS*)

If you don't feel confident that your bisexuality will be your lifelong identity, just know that you still deserve access to bi+ spaces for as long as you want or need to access them. As Lois Shearing says in *Bi the Way*:

> I just wish there were more room within queer circles to explore the possibility that some of us don't feel like we were born the way we now identify and that our sexuality may change and develop, even with our input, as we grow.[3]

If you identify as bi+ for a year, or a month, or a week or a day – your experiences should never be invalidated just because they were short-lived. They may well make up the full picture, or they could instead be a vital brush stroke on a much larger work of art.

'It's NOT a phase!'

'Okay, okay,' I hear you saying, 'I get that phases are valid. But how *likely* is it that my bisexuality is a phase? What are the cold hard stats?' Well, let's explore.

A 2008 study shows that, for most people, bisexuality isn't just a phase. Researcher Lisa Diamond tracked the labels that young non-heterosexual women (lesbian, bisexual and 'unlabelled') used to identify themselves over time. After ten years, Diamond found that 92% of the original 'bisexual' group identified as either bisexual or unlabelled. Only two people switched to a monosexual label – one to 'lesbian', one to 'heterosexual'. In fact, over the course of the ten years, more participants adopted the label 'bisexual' than ditched it![4]

This research suggests that bisexuality as 'a phase' is less common than bisexuality as a years-long, potentially lifelong, identity. My own bisexuality has remained pretty steady since I first began to get proper crushes on people, around age 11. I'm now in my late twenties, and while I've definitely questioned my sexuality over the years, each time I have, I've landed firmly back on my feet in Bi Land.

> *I didn't know bisexuality was really a thing so assumed I was gay and the 'heterosexual' feelings would go away. When I realized bisexuality was a thing, I was still acutely aware that it wouldn't be accepted, so I came out as gay at 15. I finally accepted myself at 21.* (LIBBY BAXTER-WILLIAMS (SHE/HER), BI+ COMMUNITY ADVOCATE)

We briefly touched on the #StillBisexual movement in the last chapter – a campaign created by activist and author Nicole Kristal. The #StillBisexual website details the roots of the project:

> Kristal thought if she could make folks realize the bisexual identity for most was lifelong and that bisexuals in committed monogamous relationships hadn't 'picked a side,' but instead were 'still bisexual,' perhaps some understanding could be cultivated.[5]

Kristal, and two of her friends, recorded videos of themselves, flipping handwritten cards describing their journeys with their sexuality, and asserting that their bisexuality is not a phase, but a lifelong identity to be celebrated. Soon, the campaign gained wider attention, leading to more and more people sharing videos – online celebrations of their glorious, colourful, bi+ selves.

The popularity of the movement led to features in *Cosmopolitan*, *NBC News*, *The Huffington Post*, and more. Today, the campaign has amassed an online community of over 45,000 followers across different social media platforms.[6] That's a lot of people who are pretty confident about who they are!

The #StillBisexual website features over 100 video testimonies, including a number from bisexual elders – older bi+ people, some of whom have been confident in their bisexuality since their teen years.

In one video, Dr Carol Queen recounts coming out as bisexual in 1973, when she was a student in a girls' school. Since the seventies, Carol has been a pioneer for queerness and open sexuality, authoring several books, graduating with a PhD in Sexology and curating the Antique Vibrator Museum in San Francisco – a museum dedicated to sexual liberation throughout history. (I'm a huge sex nerd so naturally, I dragged my husband here on our honeymoon!)

In another video, bi+ activist Robyn Ochs describes how she realized she was definitely bisexual just before she turned 18. Robyn has since done so much for the bi+ movement, from teaching courses on LGBTQ+ history to publishing multiple anthologies amplifying the voices of bi+ people. She was named by Teen Vogue as one of '9 bisexual women who are making history.'[7] Robyn also crafted the popular definition of bisexuality that you read in Chapter Two.

These videos from bi+ elders, many of whom have given so much back to the queer community, are inspirational and moving. I would recommend them to anyone who doubts that bisexuality can be anything more than a phase. You will see a lifetime of joy, of resilience, of queerness. You will see people who have spent decades getting to know who they are, and who now say the word 'bisexual' with their full chest, even if they once couldn't. And you have this ability within you as well, to be confident in who you are, and brush off anyone who thinks they know better.

What's the harm?

By now, I hope you know that sexuality is fluid and that some people go through phases during their self-discovery journey. So, if that's the case, what makes the 'it's just a phase' statement so harmful? Well, the issue isn't so much *what* is being said but *why* it's being said in the first place. And *what else* is being communicated in this very short sentence?

Here are some examples of the literal phrases that might be said, but what the subtext may be behind the words, or what bi+ people may interpret the statement as meaning:

What is said	What might be meant (or heard)
'It's just a phase!'	'Bisexuality isn't real.'
'You'll grow out of it.'	'You're too young to know your own mind.'
'Everyone thinks they're bi at one point or another.'	'This is only okay if it's temporary.'
'You'll pick a side eventually.'	'Any other sexuality would be better than bisexuality.'

It's possible that the parents, carers and friends of young bi+ people are reading this book, to find out how to better support a person close to them. (If this is you, you're already smashing allyship!) For a second, I'd like to speak directly to the allies: You can't know for sure whether your loved one's sexuality is a temporary phase or a permanent feature. Sometimes they won't even know themselves. But, regardless of whether or not their bi+ identity is a phase, how you react to them coming out will influence whether they figure out this part of themselves with you, or without you.

If you, upon their coming out, patronize them, disbelieve them or discourage them, one of two potential scenarios occur:

1. Your loved one, after a lot of soul-searching, realizes that bi/pan/queer isn't an accurate description of their sexuality. Having made this discovery (without your support) they are now less likely to share their new identity label with you. If this new identity is queer in any way (for example, gay, lesbian, asexual) they may fear that your reaction to *another* queer identity would be equally negative. And if they realize they're straight, they may avoid sharing this information in anticipation of an infuriating 'I told you so'.
2. Your loved one continues to identify as bi/pan/queer. The supposed 'phase' lasts their whole life. And while they might resume a relationship with you, the chances are they will always remember your initial reaction and never feel wholly accepted in their bi-ness.

But if you're supportive, no matter what the outcome, your loved one will *always* remember being listened to, believed and accepted. They'll recognize you as a safe person to be themselves with, even if that 'self' changes over the weeks, months or years.

Only you can know

Some people say that figuring out their sexuality was like a rollercoaster. In Chapter Two, I likened it to exploring a maze – not a linear or straightforward path, but one with plenty of twists and turns. At times, it might feel as if you're going back on yourself, or even that you've hit a dead end. But the reason it's a maze and not a rollercoaster is that *you* are in control. You get to plan your route, pause to take a breather, and retrace your steps as many times as you need to. You're not following a set track, you're forging your own path.

> One of the most joyful and reassuring things about being pan is knowing that you are open and alive to so much possibility – not just in terms of experiencing different partners and types of partnership, but in terms of how you express yourself and how you love. You don't just follow the manual – you write your own script. Bisexuality is an expansive superpower – by accepting it you gain so many levels of clarity and precision on who the hell YOU are. (SOPHIE DUKER (SHE/HER), COMEDIAN, WRITER AND PERFORMER)

We should never assume that someone's bisexuality is a

'stepping stone' to coming out as gay or a lesbian, because this simply isn't true for the vast majority of bi+ people. But, the reality is that this *is* the journey for some queer people – and that's okay! If this has happened to you or someone you know, it's important that you don't assume this to be a wider truth about all bi+ people. Every case is different, and every person is unique.

In 2024, singer and actor Reneé Rapp came out as a lesbian, when she had previously identified as bisexual. Many people took this public label change as permission to question and comment on Rapp's identity. From people who didn't believe she was a lesbian, to people who used her coming out as proof that bisexuality isn't real, there was *a lot* of online discourse, leading Rapp to post the following on X (formally Twitter): 'If I say I'm a lesbian I am a lesbian and if someone says they're bi they are bi. I've had enough of you witches.'[8]

In one short statement, Rapp neatly summarizes what this chapter is all about – believing people where they're at. You are allowed to question your own sexuality, others are not. If you decide that a label you've been using is no longer accurate, that only says something about *your* sexuality, not about the community as a whole.

So, if you're #StillBisexual when you're 80, that's amazing. But if bisexuality only plays a small role in your life, that's great too. Your feelings – no matter how fleeting, or complicated, or turbulent – still deserve respect. And to anyone who says otherwise, I'm channelling Reneé Rapp when I say, 'I've had enough of you witches.'

Step Bi Step...

- Young people are often the main victims of the 'it's just a phase' stereotype because bisexuality has historically been framed as an immature state that we will grow out of.
- Sexuality isn't quite as simple as being 'born this way' for lots of people. For some, it's fluid. Your bisexuality may not be lifelong and that is 100% okay!
- However, research shows us that, for most people, bisexuality is not a short-lived phase. It's important that we recognize this to avoid perpetuating the stereotype that bisexuality isn't real.
- A lot of harm can be done by the statement 'it's just a phase', even if it ends up being true! Always believe somebody where they're currently at – it's their job to question their sexuality, not yours.
- No matter how your sexuality changes or doesn't change over time, it's vital that we continue to respect people whose journey looks a bit different from ours. We're all unique, and we should all feel affirmed in our identities.

Chapter Five

Representation

'It's hard to be what you can't see.' This phrase, coined by American activist Marian Wright Edelman, succinctly captures the importance of positive representation. Bi+ people are going to be bi, pan and queer whether we see ourselves in the media or not. But the ways in which we see our identities portrayed can have a big impact on how we view ourselves, and how comfortable we feel existing openly and authentically. To paraphrase Edelman, it's hard to be a confident, proud bi+ person if you can't see confident, proud bi+ people represented in the world.

Unfortunately, the lives and experiences of bi+ people are frequently neglected in popular culture and beyond. Bi erasure – the act of denying, forgetting about or diminishing bisexuality as a sexual orientation – means that bi+ stories are rarely told, and bi+ people are seldom platformed or celebrated.

We are the invisible majority. Despite 57% of LGBTQ+ adults identifying as bi,[1] we are still forgotten and underrepresented, as people grasp for a more binary understanding of sexuality – comfortable with the opposing poles of gay and straight, oblivious to a whole world between them.

Even when bi+ people spell out our identities clearly and repeatedly, many remain unsatisfied and continue to probe, trying desperately to uncover 'the truth'. In a 1979 interview with David Bowie, interviewer Mavis Nicholson pried into his sexuality:

> Nicholson: You have been asked the question, if you are bisexual or not...
>
> Bowie: Too many times.
>
> Nicholson: Yes. And you've never quite answered it.
>
> Bowie: Oh, I have. I said I was bisexual. That's enough.
>
> Nicholson: Does that mean, though, that you really are? Or does that mean that you're keeping something...
>
> Bowie: (Interrupts) I've answered the question.[2]

Bowie is not the only celebrity whose bisexuality has been swept under the rug or mislabelled as gay. Before coming out as bisexual, Kristen Stewart's sexuality was a source of speculation for years, despite her publicly dating men and women. Seems pretty simple to me, but Stewart herself says 'It was confusing for other people'.[3] If bi+ people aren't believed when we simply say we're bisexual, you'd at least think that openly dating people of multiple genders would be enough to prove our bi-ness. Apparently not.

Widely considered a 'gay icon', Freddie Mercury's sexuality is also regularly debated by many. We know that Mercury had relationships with men and women, but for many this is merely evidence that he was a closeted gay man, rather than a bisexual one. Lesley-Ann Jones, who authored two biographies on Mercury, claims that this wasn't the case:

> It is still fascinating to me, after all these years, that Queen's management spent decades trying to convince the world that Freddie was heterosexual while he was alive, but then conceded to his homosexuality after he had died. They would not, however, allow for his bisexuality – even though they embraced and promoted Mary Austin (Mercury's longtime girlfriend) as his one true love! All their efforts to preserve Freddie in memory as, effectively, a straight man who was in love with one woman – his soulmate Mary – but who was 'corrupted' by factions of the music industry (and wasn't really gay) are ridiculous to me, he was clearly bisexual.[4]

The erasure of Mercury's sexuality once again became a talking point on the release of biopic *Bohemian Rhapsody* (2018). In one scene, Freddie admits to fiancée Mary Austin, 'I think I might be bisexual.' Austin simply stares back, before softly but confidently saying, 'Freddie, you're gay.'

This short scene shuts down any nuanced discussion of Mercury's sexuality while also implying more broadly that bi+ men are actually closeted homosexuals. Many bi+ viewers felt let down by the blatant erasure of Mercury's bisexuality, noticing that when bi+ people's stories are told, they are done so through a monosexual, binary lens. And *Bohemian Rhapsody* is just a drop in the ocean when it comes to bi erasure in the media.

Seen but not heard

Bisexual and pansexual representation on our screens is scarce. In their 2023–2024 *Where We Are On TV* report, GLAAD found that only 24% of LGBTQ+ characters across scripted broadcast, cable and streaming programming were bi+.[5] This is less than one in four queer characters, in contrast to the nearly two-thirds (57%) of the adult queer population who identify as bi.[6]

> I haven't really seen any media with bi+ representation. (JESSE (HE/HIM), AGE 17)

The BBC soap opera *EastEnders*, which first aired in the UK in 1985, has been at the forefront of many LGBTQ+ TV 'firsts', from the first gay kiss on a British soap in 1989, to the first trans character to be played by a transgender actor in a UK soap in 2015.[7]

Despite this, the show's bi+ representation hasn't quite kept up. In 2005, a storyline saw nurse Sonia Fowler cheat on her husband and commence an affair with a woman. In the years since, Sonia has continued to engage in relationships with both men and women. And while some may see this as a win for bisexuals, both *EastEnders* and Natalie Cassidy – the actress portraying Sonia – have seemed reluctant to use the B-word until recent years.

In 2020, Cassidy said, 'Sonia's dabbled – but I don't like to put a label on her sexuality, "lesbian" or "bisexual". Sonia just falls in love with human beings.'[8] Two years later, Cassidy once again avoided labelling Sonia's orientation in an interview with *The Guardian* – 'Sonia's sexuality is complicated. [...] The truth is that Sonia can fall for anyone, man or woman.'[9] It doesn't sound *that* complicated to me...

And it's not just Cassidy – viewers themselves avoid the word 'bisexual', with many labelling Sonia a 'part-time lesbian' when referring to her experiences with men and women.[10]

The 'ambiguously bi' trope (or as I like to call it, the 'I'm just into *people'* trope) refers to fictional characters who exhibit bi+ behaviour (such as flirting with, kissing or having sex with people of multiple genders) but whose sexuality is never officially labelled, leaving room for speculation. In 2019, bi activist and writer Lois Shearing created the Ramírez Test (named after actor Sara Ramírez) – a tool designed to assess the quality of bi+ representation in media. The Ramírez Test poses three questions:

1. Is the character recognizable as bisexual within the media itself?
2. Is the character's bisexuality presented as a joke or flaw?
3. Does the character ever say that they're bi/pansexual?[11]

Otherwise positive representations of bi+ people often fail the test at the third question. Many seemingly bisexual characters refute labels, claiming to 'just love people'. This is an entirely valid way to define your sexuality, but when it is the only media representation of multi-gender attraction, it raises questions as to why the word 'bisexual' is avoided at all costs.

> *My favourite bisexual representation is the characters from* The Picture of Dorian Gray*. Every main character in that book is arguably bisexual.* (CHARLIE (HE/HIM), AGE 17)

In Shearing's initial article explaining the Ramírez Test, they share a Tumblr post in which one user jokes, 'What's the difference between bi people and unicorns? I can see unicorns on movies and TV.' A second user comments, 'Also, unicorns on TV are called unicorns, not "horses that don't like labels".'[12]

In June 2023, *EastEnders* finally labelled Sonia's sexuality as bisexual. When the topic of her ex-girlfriend arises at a dinner party, taking new boyfriend Reiss by surprise, Sonia turns to him and casually states, 'I'm bisexual; I thought you knew that.' It feels as if this statement is directed not only to Reiss, but to the viewer – an attempt to put years of speculation and mislabelling to bed.

This declaration came only a few years after BBC drama boss, Oliver Kent, and *EastEnders* scriptwriter, Pete Lawson, admitted that they needed to do better when it came to bisexual representation. At a panel event on LGBTQ inclusion, Kent commented, 'I think that something we could be better at exploring is bisexual characters. I don't think we've quite got that right yet as often as we could.'[13] In response, Lawson addressed the show's reluctance to label its characters as bi, 'We're not brilliant at having characters who go, "I am bisexual, I love men and women."'[14]

While Lawson's comment predates Shearing's Ramírez Test, it refers to the same type of bi erasure. Broadcasting bi+ stories and experiences (fictional or real) is only one step towards good representation. The next step is to create nuanced and authentic bi+ characters, who don't fall into the same reductive and harmful tropes.

Are we the bad guys?

Unfortunately, depictions of bisexuality are often caricatures – our identities reduced to (overwhelmingly negative) tropes or stereotypes. When we do see ourselves on screen, our identities are presented as a topic of debate, as demeaning, or even as unlikeable or villainous.

One such negative depiction is of bisexual people as sexually promiscuous and greedy. This is sometimes referred to as the 'anything that moves' trope, where a character's bisexuality is simply a side effect of their flirtatious personality and lack of sexual boundaries.

My first exposure to a bisexual character falls into this category. I was nine when my dad introduced me to *Doctor Who*. I swiftly developed a little baby crush on the charismatic time-traveller Captain Jack Harkness, trying not to blush in front of my dad as I watched him flirt with Rose Tyler. I remember being surprised when, throughout the series, Harkness's flirting extended to both women and men. In one episode, he kisses both Rose and The Doctor goodbye on the lips, the latter marking the show's first same-sex kiss.

I remember questioning this at the time. 'Is he gay?' I asked my dad. (I'm hoping you can excuse such problematic bi erasure, given that I was, y'know, nine.) 'No,' my dad said, 'he'll just go for anything that moves.'

To be clear, there's absolutely nothing wrong with being sexually adventurous, or having multiple sexual or romantic partners. But when bisexual people are frequently portrayed as promiscuous, with no sexual boundaries, this perpetuates a stereotype that just isn't an accurate representation of many bi+ people.

Other bi+ people, especially women, are depicted as manipulative and dangerous. This trope is sometimes referred to as the 'depraved bisexual' or 'bisexual femme fatale' trope. Villanelle from *Killing Eve* is an example of this – a violent and highly skilled assassin who will have sex with anyone, of any gender, as a means to an end. She seduces them, and then she kills them.

This trope furthers the idea that bisexuality is a manipulation tactic, something that is switched on when it is convenient and advantageous to the bi+ person. It paints bisexuals as untrustworthy, and self-serving.

Many of the harmful or inaccurate myths we've covered in previous chapters are also perpetuated in the media. The stereotype of bisexuality as a phase comes up again and again in film and television – *Scott Pilgrim vs. the Word*

(2010) is probably one of the most on-the-nose examples. Scott is stunned when he finds out that his crush, Ramona, has an ex-girlfriend. 'You and her?' he asks. 'It was just a phase,' Ramona replies. If this weren't bad enough, Scott responds by saying, 'You had a sexy phase?' (This is classic fetishization, which we'll explore more in Chapter Seven.)

Sex and the City fuels phallocentric ideas about bisexuality when Carrie debates whether or not to continue a relationship with a bi man. 'Y'know, I did the "date the bisexual guy" thing in college,' she says to her friends. 'But in the end, they all ended up with men.' The other women nod knowingly, before Samantha adds, 'So did the bisexual women.'

If that's not enough harmful bisexual stereotyping for one coffee with the girls, Carrie goes on, 'I'm not even sure bisexuality exists. I think it's just a layover on the way to Gaytown.' Of the four women, Samantha is the only one who encourages Carrie to continue dating the man in question, while Miranda exclaims, 'It's greedy! He's double-dipping!' and Charlotte adds that people should 'pick a side and stay there'.

And while it's true that these examples are from 10–20 years ago, problematic representations of bisexuality persist on TV today. *Big Mouth*, an otherwise queer-inclusive Netflix show about teenagers going through puberty, introduces a pansexual character – Ali – in season three who quickly claims that bisexuality is a trans-exclusionary identity (a myth we debunked in Chapter Three). In front of the class, Ali explains her sexuality as 'into boys, girls and everyone in between' to which classmate Nick queries, 'I thought that was bisexual?' Exasperated, Ali says, 'No. Bisexuality is so binary' before using a metaphor to explain that bisexuals like men and women but pansexual people are also into trans men and women, as well as non-binary people.

While *Big Mouth* definitely missed the mark here, the show does get bi+ representation right in many other ways. Not only does it create space for a number of bi and pan characters within its cast, but these characters feel fleshed out and feature in storylines that span beyond their sexual orientation.

Bi+ representation is slowly getting better. The quantity of bi+ characters is improving, and so is the quality. We're increasingly seeing accurate and inclusive portrayals of bisexuality – characters whose bi-ness is a core part of their identity, but not the only noteworthy thing about them. The caricatures are being left behind, and bi+ characters are finally being afforded the nuance and sensitivity that they deserve.

Positive representation (at last!)

When bi+ representation is done right, it can feel like a

release of tension. I've grown so accustomed to seeing my identity as the subject of debate, or as wrong or manipulative in some way, that to see multidimensional bisexual and pansexual characters thrive feels like a warm hug.

I'd like to share some characters who make me feel this way. They're not perfect – that's not the point – but they're real, and they show bisexuality in a broadly positive light, without glossing over or ignoring the challenges that bi+ people face in our daily lives. (Spoilers ahead!)

Darryl Whitefeather (*Crazy Ex-Girlfriend*)

Darryl Whitefeather passes the Ramírez Test's third question with flying pink, purple and blue colours – not only saying he's bi, but singing it! When Darryl comes out to his co-workers as bisexual, it's through a musical number – 'Gettin' Bi' – in which the character does some myth-debunking of his own, declaring through song that he's confident in his sexuality, and that it isn't a phase.

Following his coming out, Darryl enters into a same-sex relationship for several of the show's seasons, but his attraction to people of different genders isn't forgotten (as happens to so many bi+ characters). By the *Crazy Ex-Girlfriend* finale, Darryl is in a happy relationship with a woman and they're expecting a child together.

Rosa Diaz (*Brooklyn Nine-Nine*)

Detective Rosa Diaz is a bi icon for so many people, as is the actress who plays her, Stephanie Beatriz. Rosa comes out as bisexual to her friends in the police squad in the fifth season of *Brooklyn Nine-Nine*. After coming out, Rosa clearly states her boundaries by allowing only 60 seconds for questions, before swiftly getting back to work.

Following a positive reception from her colleagues, Rosa is then faced with the challenge of coming out to her conservative parents, which doesn't go quite as smoothly. However, she's supported by her friends – a beautiful example of chosen family. The storyline was inspired by Beatriz' own experiences, and this shines through in the full, rich character of Rosa.

> *I love Captain Holt and Rosa Diaz from Brooklyn Nine-Nine – for me it was the first time I was able to see LGBTQIA+ characters be badasses and great, without being limited to their sexuality, yet still embracing it. They were a real inspiration and made discovering my sexuality a lot easier.* (JOHN (HE/HIM), AGE 16)

David Rose (*Schitt's Creek*)

Many bi+ people are familiar with the wine metaphor used to describe David's sexuality in *Schitt's Creek*. David is shopping for wine with his friend Stevie, who he has recently had sex with, when she subtly broaches the topic of David's sexuality.

She says, 'I only drink red wine. And up until last night I was under the impression that you too only drank red wine. But I guess I was wrong?' David, picking up on the metaphor, replies, 'I do drink red wine. But I also drink white wine. And I've been known to sample the occasional rosé. And a couple summers back I tried a Merlot that used to be a Chardonnay.' Stevie responds, 'Yeah, so you're just really open to all wines' to which David says, 'I like the wine and not the label.'

While this may seem on the surface to be another example of not explicitly naming a non-monosexual identity, David's orientation is labelled as pansexual later in the same episode.

Nick Nelson (*Heartstopper*)

Heartstopper is the queer series I wish I'd had when I was 13. It follows teenage boys Nick and Charlie as they start to date and fall in love. While Charlie already knows that he is gay, Nick's feelings for Charlie cause him to question his identity. In one very relatable scene he takes 'Am I Gay?' quizzes online – a true flashback to my own teen years.

> *My favourite bi representation is Nick Nelson in Heartstopper, because his journey to figuring out his sexuality is quite realistic and shows that it's okay not to know your identity immediately.* (THEO (HE/HIM), AGE 14)

Nick realizes he is bisexual and eventually comes out to his mum in a heartfelt, tender scene at the kitchen table. His mum hugs him, tells him she loves him, and then adds, 'You don't have to say that you like girls if you don't.' What I love about this scene is Nick's mum's assurance that she'll accept Nick no matter who he likes or doesn't like, but when he reiterates that he definitely still likes girls, she believes him wholeheartedly, validating and accepting his bisexuality.

Adam Groff (*Sex Education*)

One of my favourite TV shows of all time, *Sex Education* has a plethora of bisexual, pansexual and queer characters, including Adam Groff – a school bully with some deep-seated internalized queerphobia. Throughout the first season, we see Adam making classmate Eric the target of his homophobic abuse before they eventually kiss in the season finale.

When Adam comes out to Eric as bisexual in season two, Eric is supportive, but ultimately lets Adam know that this is no excuse for the way he's behaved in the past. Thus begins Adam's journey of striving to be a better person to others, while working on his own self-hatred. Despite Adam's problematic start, I think he's one of my favourite characters in the show – he illustrates just how damaging internalized queerphobia can be, not only to ourselves but to our LGBTQIA+ peers.

Positive representation doesn't mean characters with no flaws, who never do anything wrong. It means characters who don't feel tokenistic, or whose identity isn't entirely dependent on stereotypes. They're characters you root for, and see elements of yourself in. Characters who feel real.

> *Heartbreak High* and *Young Royals* literally have such good representation and I love those shows so, so much. (TESS (SHE/HER), AGE 16)

You have the power to be selective with the media you consume, to turn off the TV when a depiction of queerness makes you feel uncomfortable, or makes you question the validity of your own identity. Be intentional with your attention, take recommendations from other bi+ friends and invest in stories that not only feature bi+ characters, but that have bi+ creatives bringing the story to life. Trust me when I say that you'll notice the difference.

And if you see bisexuality or pansexuality depicted negatively, stereotypically, or in a way that spreads harmful misinformation, let the creators know! You could email the streaming platform, post on social media and tag the actors/writers, or give the show/film/book a negative review online, explaining clearly why you, as a bi+ person, didn't enjoy this content.

Better representation relies on people calling out bad representation and clearly stating the impact it has on bi+ people. Media has the potential to shape our attitudes towards the people we encounter in real life – if all bisexuals are depicted as manipulative, non-committal and self-indulgent, then it's no surprise when biphobia doesn't stay contained to our screens, and seeps its way into the real world.

Step Bi Step...

- Bi+ people lack representation in the media – our sexualities are either unlabelled, or mislabelled as straight or gay. 'Bisexual' and 'pansexual' seem to be dirty words that writers shy away from using to describe characters who experience attraction to multiple genders.

- Depictions of bi+ people often rely on negative stereotypes – we are painted as promiscuous, untrustworthy or manipulative. This is harmful, and reinforces biphobic attitudes towards bi+ people.

- Increasingly, TV shows and movies are getting bi+ representation right. Positive representation involves characters who are non-tokenistic, aren't reliant on tropes and who feel authentic to the viewer.

- The media we consume has an impact on how we feel about ourselves. Avoid media that makes you feel ashamed, and seek out films, TV shows and books that nourish your identity.

Chapter Six

Biphobia

The trouble with viewing bisexuality as a 'diet' brand of other sexualities – half-gay or half-straight – is that what follows is the assumption that our hardships, the discrimination we face, equally come in half measures; that because we're not 'fully gay' we don't face the same level of homophobic oppression as 'fully' gay and lesbian people; that we have an easier ride because we have at least one foot in 'heterosexuality'; that we're at least partially shielded from the onslaught of abuse that LGBTQIA+ people battle against every day.

This simply isn't true. Bi+ people – our challenges, our culture, our complexities – do not exist in a vacuum, but we *are* unique. We do not endure identical forms of discrimination to gay and lesbian people, but nor do we experience diluted oppression. If bisexuality is defined as attraction to more than one gender, then biphobia could very well be defined as exposure to more than one form of queerphobia.

The first thing to establish is that biphobia is not homophobia simply directed towards bi+ people. Homophobia refers to prejudice or discrimination towards people who experience same-gender attraction. Put very simply, it's the belief that boys shouldn't kiss boys, and girls shouldn't kiss girls. Homophobia affects anybody who fancies someone of the same gender as themselves – including gay men, lesbians and bi+ people.

But biphobia (sometimes referred to as monosexism) is the belief that being attracted to *more than one* gender is wrong. It's not about boys making out with boys, it's about boys making out with boys *and* girls *and* people of other genders. Biphobia demands exclusivity in the gender you're attracted to, no matter which gender that is.

Now, lots of people are both homophobic and biphobic – they believe that any type of queerness is wrong. Some people, however, are fully on board with gay and lesbian relationships, but seem to draw the line at bisexuality. I can't count the number of times I've heard someone pledge their support to the gay and lesbian community, claiming 'love is love', but then recoil at the mention of bisexuality – 'there's nothing wrong with being gay, but that's just greedy' – as if we simply need to exercise more self-control than other queers.

Biphobia is vast. It can rear its head when you least expect it and punch you square in the gut. It's in our healthcare, our schools, our workplaces and, as seen from the previous chapter, our media. It's everywhere and it has the power to cause irreversible harm – but to figure out the solution, we first need to understand the problem.

A shock to the system

When we talk about systemic biphobia, we refer to the ways in which biphobic attitudes and bi erasure are ingrained into the very fabric of our society. Our world is made up of systems – like healthcare, education and the law – that are not built with bi+ people in mind. When this happens, bi+ people are regularly mistreated, neglected or simply forgotten. Sometimes this erasure is unintentional, and comes from a lack of education; other times it is a deliberate attempt to exclude us.

Education and the workplace

Talking about homosexuality in schools used to be illegal in the UK. In 1988, Margaret Thatcher's Conservative government introduced Section 28 – a law that banned local authorities and schools from 'promoting homosexuality'. The legislation prevented councils from funding any materials depicting same-sex relationships – including books, films and leaflets – and stopped teachers from educating students about gay relationships.[1]

This law left teachers unable to support queer students without risking their jobs, and reinforced the idea that gayness was in some way immoral. Thatcher famously said: 'Children who need to be taught to respect traditional moral values are being taught that they have an inalienable right to be gay. All of those children are being cheated of a sound start in life.'[2]

Section 28 was repealed in 2000 in Scotland, but not until 2003 in England and Wales. My own first few years of school were under this homophobic legislation.

Despite the shadow left by Section 28, today many schools in the UK recognize and address the needs of LGBTQIA+ students. But for lots of these schools, steps to include gay and lesbian experiences in the curriculum often end up reinforcing a binary that leaves bi+ people out of the conversation.

Three in four LGBT pupils (76%) report having never learned about bisexuality at school.[3] Think back to any sex and relationships education you might have had – perhaps, in an effort to be inclusive, your teacher may have said something like, 'You need to use contraception, regardless of if you're gay or straight.' (*What if you're bisexual?*) Or 'This information is important whether you date boys or girls.' (*What if I date both?*)

This binary thinking might even extend to a school's approach to combating discrimination. Many schools teach students about the harmful effects of homophobia, and the impact it has on gay and lesbian students. Biphobia, meanwhile, goes unremarked on, slipping silently under the radar.

One participant in a Stonewall research study said of their school: 'Homophobic language and sexist language are not tolerated, which is great. But I'm bisexual. I find that biphobic remarks are brushed off and aren't treated anywhere near as seriously.'[4]

According to research by Stonewall, 47% of bisexual students have received negative comments from other students because they're bi, and 7% have been physically attacked. In many cases, this behaviour goes unreported, with 33% of bi students saying that they would not feel comfortable reporting biphobic bullying and harassment to their educational institution.[5]

> Personally, I have never been picked on for my sexuality; however, I know people who have and how it can affect them. The person I knew got through it by talking to a teacher, so that's what I would recommend doing if any bullying ever happens to you or people you know. I know that it can be hard to get through being bullied, but stay strong and stick up for yourself and you'll come through the other end stronger! (CAITLIN (SHE/HER), AGE 13)

For many, the fear of biphobia stays with us when we leave

school and move on to higher education. While 44% of gay and lesbian uni students are out to everyone at their university, the same can only be said for 23% of bi+ people.[6]

But why do students feel unable to come out? Possibly because academia doesn't make space for bi+ identities. Many academic resources are dominated by straight, white men, leaving women, People of Colour and LGBTQIA+ folk feeling unrepresented within the curriculum. In a 2021 article, psychology student Thomas York remarked on the lack of bi representation in academia:

> While I am yet to reach my final year of study, I do not feel represented in the curriculum so far. We're talking about one of the most prominent areas of psychology, human relationships, yet much of the classic research ignores or erases my experiences. It's time for bisexuality to stand as a unique identity.[7]

Sadly, binary thinking and biphobic attitudes aren't necessarily left behind once you leave education. For some bi+ people, the workplace presents another minefield of monosexism, despite legal protections around discrimination and company diversity programmes. As with schools, we find that workplace LGBT inclusion often focuses on gay and lesbian issues, with bisexual activist Marcus Morgan saying: 'Most workplace LGBT networks are primarily lesbian and gay networks. Bisexual people have reported being made to feel unwelcome if they bring opposite sex partners to supposedly inclusive events.'[8]

This specific type of hostility reinforces the idea that your queerness is only valid when you're dating someone of the same sex – completely untrue.

Once again, a system has been created where bi+ people feel unsafe coming out to colleagues: 38% of bisexuals aren't out to anyone in the workplace; compared to 7% of gay men and 4% of lesbians, that's staggering.[9]

In workplaces where biphobia is a problem, bi+ people may avoid coming out in case it negatively impacts their career, costing them opportunities, promotions or even their job. While many countries have legal protections in place to ensure that nobody can be fired due to their sexuality, this doesn't always help the fear that some bi+ people live with on a daily basis.

As with school, when bullying and harassment does occur, bi+ people are far less likely to report it than their gay and lesbian colleagues. Only 28% of bisexuals said they would feel confident reporting discriminatory behaviour compared to 41% of gay and lesbian people.[10]

Knowing your rights in education and the workplace is the first step in advocating for yourself if you're ever made to feel uncomfortable or discriminated against. Many schools and businesses will have LGBT inclusion policies that you, as a student or employee, have a right to access. If you read these policies and notice that bi+ people and biphobia aren't addressed, raise this with your teacher or employer. The ability to thrive within our work or our studies is often dependent on how safe and supported we feel within our environment.

Healthcare

I used to work for the National LGBT Partnership, an LGBT health charity, researching and advocating for queer people's health and wellbeing. My time there was eye-opening, especially when it came to bi+ people's experiences of the healthcare system.

It's undeniable that healthcare services are largely heteronormative, with queer people experiencing a worse quality of treatment and a lack of understanding surrounding their identities. And while many healthcare facilities have made progress in understanding same-sex attraction and relationships, the system is still a binary one, where people who don't fall into the categories of 'gay' or 'straight' instead fall right through the cracks.

One study by the National LGBT Partnership found that over a quarter (27%) of bi+ people had experienced unequal treatment due to their sexual orientation[11] – being shamed by medical staff, having assumptions made about their sex lives, or being mislabelled on forms as 'heterosexual' or 'gay' depending on their current partner's gender.

Even when doctors and nurses have good intentions, many bi+ patients are made to feel uncomfortable. Often, a lack of LGBTQIA+ awareness training means that healthcare workers don't know what's appropriate to ask when a patient comes out, and 28% of bi+ people reported experiencing inappropriate curiosity about their sexuality in a healthcare setting.[12]

It can feel uncomfortable when questions are being asked from a place of nosiness, and not because they're relevant to your health. For example, 'Are you having sex with multiple partners?' would be a reasonable question to be asked in a sexual health appointment – less so when you're seeking treatment for a broken leg. (Top tip: 'Can I ask why you need that information?' is a powerful question. Use it.)

This lack of education and awareness makes bi+ people fearful of coming out to their healthcare providers at all. A study by Stonewall found that 40% of bi men and 29% of bi women aren't out to anyone when seeking medical care, compared to only 10% of gay men and 11% of lesbians.[13] Clearly, this is a bi thing.

It's to be expected that the topic of our sexuality may arise when seeking care for our sexual health. Accessing sexual health services is important (more on this in Chapter Ten) but it often requires being upfront about the types of sex you're having, and with whom. And while many sexual health nurses are incredible and have gone through *extensive* LGBTQIA+ training, some clinics still aren't totally up to date on how to provide an inclusive and non-judgemental service to bi+ people.

Some bi+ people report nurses making assumptions and falling over themselves to offer testing for a full range of sexually transmitted infections (STIs), even when the person in question isn't having sex at the time. This often only arises after they come out as bi, with limited, or no, STI testing offered beforehand.[14]

Bi+ women report receiving misinformation about their risk of getting STIs – told that as long as they're only having sex with people with vulvas, they don't need to use contraception or get tested. (This is very much not true!)[15]

HIV is a treatable, but incurable, STI that can be passed on during unprotected sex. Some HIV services try to spread the message that men who have sex with men are at a higher risk of contracting the infection, but in classic bi erasure style, completely forget that bi men exist. One participant for a National LGBT Partnership study said: 'When it comes to support services, it's always been that there is a gay men's service and a straight group. So, if you are HIV positive and bisexual, you have to pick.'[16]

As a result, some research suggests that bisexual men are likely to have less knowledge about HIV than gay men, and are also less likely to get tested.[17] It's all just one big biphobic domino effect.

And while sexual health services may be the go-to for our physical sexual wellbeing, our sexuality can also have an impact on our minds. Mental health services are often a safe haven for LGBTQIA+ people in the midst of figuring out their sexuality, and therapy can be a great place to explore and discuss your feelings in confidence. Yet encounters with therapists who are ignorant of bi+ identities, or have personal biases against bisexuality, can instead make our mental health worse, not better. Bi+ people report appointments with therapists where their sexuality is called into question – seen as a riddle to be solved.[18]

Conversion therapy is the practice of trying to change somebody's sexuality, usually from queer to straight. You might be picturing religious conversion camps, where young people are sent away against their will to be 'cured' of their queerness. But sometimes conversion therapy is more subtle than that. Bi+ people have recounted experiences where a therapist treated their bisexuality as a flaw, the root cause of their unhappiness, even when the person in question insisted that their sexuality wasn't an issue for them.

Some therapists have implied that patients' bisexuality shows an unstable sense of self, and that true happiness cannot be achieved until the individual 'picks a side' – gay or straight. In a National LGBT Partnership research report, one bi+ person said:

> I've had therapists literally tell me that I only think I'm bisexual, but I'm actually straight or actually gay because of something that happened in my childhood. [...] I've quit two therapies because every session was just over and over about trying to cure my bisexual behaviour.[19]

Bisexuality is pathologized, meaning that instead of being viewed as a harmless part of someone's identity, it is instead seen as a symptom of a wider issue with one's mental health. Something to be cured, rather than something to be celebrated.

But with more healthcare workers receiving training on queer identities, including bisexuality, there is hope that the quality of our care will continue to improve, and the system will adapt to accommodate and uplift people beyond the binary of gay and straight.

The law

In many countries around the world, there are legal rights that protect LGBTQIA+ people. For example, the 2010

Equality Act in the UK protects homosexual and bisexual citizens from discrimination on the basis of their sexuality.

Yet, even when bi+ rights are written into law, they are usually grouped together with the rights of lesbian and gay people. On one hand, this makes sense, as we share a common enemy in homophobic discrimination. But, as we know, many bi+ people are also victims of biphobia and experience unique challenges that aren't shared by monosexual queer people. Once again, the distinct types of oppression that we experience aren't recognized in all of their nuances.

The law repeatedly lets down bi+ people, despite its pledge to protect us. Take the case of Javier Vilalta, a Spanish human rights lawyer who had been amicably separated from his wife for over a decade when she tried to sue him for €10,000 in 2020. The grounds? That he had concealed his homosexuality from her during their marriage, using her to maintain the appearance of a heterosexual man. Except, Vilalta isn't gay – he's bisexual.

In an incredibly expensive act of bi erasure, a judge ruled in favour of his ex-wife, claiming that she would never have entered the marriage in the first place if she knew his 'true sexuality'. Vilalta was ordered to pay his ex-wife a total of €3,000 – €1,000 for every year they were married.[20]

Vilalta appealed the court's ruling and, fortunately, Spain's high court overturned the decision, stating that the initial ruling was discriminatory and an invasion of privacy. While this was a great win for Vilalta, much of the damage could not be undone. 'The trial has been shameful,' he said, and described the initial sentence as 'a slap in the face'.[21]

Like in Vilalta's case, the misconception that bisexuals are untrustworthy, manipulative liars seeps into the legal system and can have a profound impact on the lives of bi+ people. In countries where same-sex relationships are illegal, the stakes are sometimes life or death, leading queer people to seek asylum elsewhere.

In these incredibly difficult and emotional circumstances, being bisexual can actually make things even trickier. In their book *Bi the Way*, Lois Shearing explains:

> Many asylum processes require proof that the claimant is gay, which is difficult to prove at the best of times, but impossible if you're not actually gay, because you're bi. In multiple cases, claimants' previous different-gender relationships have been used to deny their claims, with many bi (and gay) asylum seekers being told that they should return to their country of origin and pass as straight.[22]

To avoid this, bisexual asylum seekers are often encouraged to claim a gay identity. This not only erases and de-legitimizes bi+ people and their experiences, but also has the potential to jeopardize their whole case if this is found to be untrue.

We have a long way to go in securing the rights of bi+ people in law. Even when, on paper, we seem to be protected, it is obvious that human bias and a lack of knowledge about bisexuality are standing in our way to true equality.

The LGBTQIA+ community

The LGBTQIA+ community is a marginalized group in and of itself. Queer people have been persecuted by broader society for centuries, and as such, our community has a long, proud history of fighting back against oppression. However, this doesn't mean that we are free from discrimination and social hierarchies within our own circles.

Biphobic attitudes held by monosexual queer people are reflected in the broader LGBT sphere, with 27% of bi women and 18% of bi men reporting that they've experienced discrimination from others in the community. For comparison, the same was true for only 9% of lesbians and 4% of gay men.[23]

A 2008 study by Kirsten McLean explored bisexual men and women's experiences of Australia's gay and lesbian scene, and found that anti-bisexual attitudes were rife, having a profound impact on bi+ people's willingness to access queer spaces, and their experiences when they do. One research participant said:

> My experiences have been mixed. They range from completely accepting to nonchalant to condescending and patronising. I've had comments like I'm 'just confused', 'it's just a phase', 'come back when you've sorted yourself out'.[24]

McLean notes the history of biphobia in the Australian LGBT scene. The Sydney Gay and Lesbian Mardi Gras, which began as a protest march in 1978, adopted new guidelines for membership in 1996 following a rise in homophobic violence at the parade and after-parties. As part of the new guidelines, their membership form was updated to include tick boxes for applicants' sexual orientation and gender identity:

> If applicants ticked the boxes marked 'gay,' 'lesbian,' 'homosexual,' or 'transgender,' they were automatically granted membership. However, if applicants ticked the boxes marked 'heterosexual,' 'bisexual,' 'queer,' or 'choose not to identify,' they would be required to 'provide supplementary information justifying their application.'[25]

Many people who ticked 'bisexual' were not granted Mardi Gras membership. And while bi+ people no longer need to physically tick a box to prove we're queer enough to attend Pride, the sentiment still hangs in the air 30 years later.

Every summer, without fail, the annual discussion ignites

again surrounding bi+ people's place at Pride. If you're like me and spend hours doomscrolling on social media, you've possibly seen it for yourself. Gay and lesbian people, our supposed allies, make videos and posts warning bisexual people (often women) that if they're in a straight-presenting relationship, their partner is not welcome at Pride.

Pride has always welcomed respectful allies, and many monosexual queer people are accompanied by cishet friends and family members with no issues. But for bi+ people, suddenly our biggest allies – our partners – are not welcome. Some people even go as far as to say that bi+ people themselves shouldn't come to Pride if they have the 'privilege' of being in a 'straight' relationship.

This specific type of biphobia seems mostly targeted towards bi and pan women, likely fuelled by the 'bisexual women aren't really bi' myth. We're only embraced at Pride once we're perceived to be queer enough by our gay and lesbian peers. Ironic, given that Brenda Howard – the woman responsible for the very first Pride parade – often called the 'Mother of Pride', was bisexual.[26]

> *Most of the biphobia I've experienced has been bi erasure – people deciding my sexuality for me or fully denying that bisexuality exists – it's honestly exhausting.* (TOMMY (HE/HIM), AGE 14)

With so many bi+ people made to feel unsafe in

predominantly heterosexual environments, it's vital that we have access to spaces where our queerness, and specifically our bisexuality, is accepted. The rise of Pride festivals, queer venues and LGBT book clubs should be a beacon of light for bi+ people and yet 43% of bi people say that they've never attended an LGBT space or event. Only 29% of gay and lesbian people said the same.[27]

In a National LGBT Partnership study, one participant said: 'I think what these spaces don't understand is that with biphobia, the call often comes from within the house, within our own community. I don't think they understand. It's like missiles from both sides'.[28]

Queer spaces have a responsibility to tackle biphobia that happens inside their walls, to create an environment where all LGBTQIA+ people feel welcome, and where nobody has to flash their 'queer enough' ID at the door.

The impact

So, when biphobia seems to be, well, everywhere, what is the impact on bi+ people? How does it affect our day-to-day lives?

'Minority stress' describes chronic stress experienced by members of marginalized groups, as a result of prejudice, discrimination and navigating a world that wasn't built with them in mind. While everyone, no matter how privileged, experiences some level of stress – sick relatives, busy schedules, money worries – people from minority or marginalized groups have to put up with all of that and more. For bi+ people, this additional stress looks like everything you've just read in this chapter.

And minority stress has a real impact on our health and wellbeing. The 2021 UK census found that 76% of the UK population reported being in good health,[29] while a study from the National LGBT Partnership found that only 51% of bi+ people reported the same.[30]

The difference can really be seen in our emotional wellbeing, and the degree to which bi+ people are affected by poor mental health. According to a 2020 Stonewall study, 59% of bi+ people reported experiencing depression in the year prior to the study, compared to 46% of gay and lesbian respondents. Additionally, half of bi+ people felt that life wasn't worth living (for gay and lesbian people this was 35%) and over one in four had self-harmed (compared to one in ten gay and lesbian respondents).[31] Other studies have found that thoughts of suicide[32] and substance misuse[33] are higher in bi+ people than in other sexual minority groups.

But the impact isn't contained to our mental health, with research suggesting that bisexuals' physical health may also suffer, likely due to biphobia in healthcare services causing bi+ people to avoid going to the doctor altogether. Certain types of cancer, such as cervical and breast cancer, have been reported at higher rates in bisexual and lesbian women, in part as a result of the misguided and dangerous advice that women who have sex with women don't need to get cervical screenings.[34]

It may feel dramatic to say that biphobia is killing us, but in so many ways it is. What may seem like an ignorant, offhand joke about bisexuals actually feeds larger and more vicious types of oppression that leave us with mental and physical scars. When we fight back against biphobia, we don't just fight for the right to love who we love, we fight for our lives.

Dealing with biphobia

'Help, now I feel really panicked/depressed/hopeless!'

Yep, this chapter was a heavy one. But all hope is not lost. If I thought nothing could be done, I wouldn't be sitting here writing a book – I'd be crying under my duvet eating chocolate and watching *Friends* for the millionth time. But I believe in change and, more importantly, I believe that you can play a part in making that change happen.

So before we leave this gloomy chapter behind, I want to share with you the ways in which you personally can combat biphobia and protect yourself a little from its effects. Read this section and then go and practise some post-biphobia-chat self-care, in the knowledge that you have what it takes to push our world in a better direction.

Find your people

Never underestimate the value of venting to other bi+ people who really *get it*. If you already have bi, pan and queer besties, that's amazing. But if not, there are people out there who want to be your friend. Join an LGBTQIA+ youth group, or follow and (safely) connect with bi+ accounts online. Sometimes a good bisexuality meme is all I need to feel fully seen.

Tackle misinformation

If you feel safe and comfortable in doing so, combat harmful stereotypes of bisexuality head-on. Maybe that looks like calling out a friend the next time they make a flippant comment about bi+ people being sluts. If your school has a serious problem with biphobia, you could ask your teacher to hire an external bi+ speaker to give a talk. (I'm available for hire...) Perhaps you make an online video series debunking common misconceptions about bisexuality. Be loud, demanding and audacious.

Report it!

If you're experiencing biphobic bullying in school or at work, or have witnessed somebody else going through this, you can report it. Lots of schools and workplaces have policies in place to help address and combat the prejudice and discrimination experienced by LGBTQIA+ people.

Speaking to a teacher or your boss can be scary, but their role is to protect you and the other people in their care. You don't even have to come out to them as bi+ if you don't want to. You could simply say, 'I've observed a lot of biphobia recently which doesn't make for a safe environment for bi+ students/employees.' Play the role of Concerned Ally if you need to!

In countries like the UK and the USA, LGBT people are protected by law. Anti-LGBT hate crime – when somebody is the victim of abuse or violence because of their sexual orientation of gender identity – is illegal. Hate crimes aren't limited to violence and can include verbal threats, online bullying or damage to property. You always have the right to report anti-LGBT abuse to the police.

Look after your mental health

Mental health is no joke. If you're starting to feel that your wellbeing is suffering because of biphobia, then it's time to talk to somebody. There are services out there that support LGBTQIA+ young people in accessing mental health care, and helplines if you're feeling as if you need to talk to someone urgently (check out the Further Support section at the end of this book).

You can also talk to your doctor. Even if you're underage, you have a right to confidentiality and your doctor cannot legally disclose your sexual orientation to anybody, including your parents.

Ask, 'What is in my control?'

I'm sure we'd all love to bring an end to biphobia but hey, bisexual utopia wasn't built in a day. While joining a protest or celebrating your identity at Pride is amazing and worthwhile, it's not a quick fix, and you might want some more short-term hacks to filter the biphobia out of your life. When it all gets a bit too much, ask yourself, 'What's in my control, and what isn't?'

You can't control what people say or do. You can't prevent harmful stereotypes of bi+ people from making their way into the media. You can't make your family understand you if they're not willing to learn. There is so much you can't control and I know how helpless that might make you feel.

But there is so, so much that you *can* control. You can take a social media break if the biphobia gets too much online. You can block people who say or repost harmful things. You can turn off the news. You can choose to spend time with people who make you feel safe and affirmed in who you are. You can read books, or watch TV shows, or listen to music that celebrates bisexuality and find comfort in characters who are just like you. You can lose yourself in a pastime that you enjoy – be it skateboarding, crocheting or gardening. You can exist in the world as a creative, complex, thoughtful, messy, radiant bi+ person and know that that in itself is a form of protest and rebellion.

> My favourite thing about being bisexual is the way bisexuality allows me to think about and understand social power and oppression, and then resist it. For example, the stereotype that we're indecisive tells me that society is afraid of destabilizing binary sexual categories. The stereotype that we're sluts tells me it's afraid of sexual independence and agency. When we know these things, we can resist them together, and use bisexuality as a tool to fight against oppression and work towards liberation. (SHIRI EISNER (SHE/THEY), ACTIVIST, WRITER AND AUTHOR OF *BI: NOTES FOR A BISEXUAL REVOLUTION*)

Step Bi Step...

- Biphobia and homophobia are two different beasts, and bi+ people often fight against them both.

- Biphobia is systemic, and appears in the foundations of many areas in our lives – from healthcare to education to the law, and even within LGBTQIA+ spaces themselves.

- Minority stress is the direct result of biphobia and can have a profound effect on our mental and physical wellbeing as bi+ people.

- You are not powerless! There are so many things you can do to combat biphobia, and to look after yourself when you're feeling the sting of oppression. Change is happening, and you get to be a part of it.

Chapter Seven

Intersectional Identities

Bi+ people are not a homogeneous group. While we may have a lot in common – for example, we all experience biphobic oppression – there are other factors in our lives and identities which mean that our experiences can also differ, sometimes drastically.

Intersectionality, a term coined by Kimberlé Crenshaw in 1989,[1] describes how people who hold multiple marginalized identities experience oppression in unique and blended ways. We know that bi+ people may lack privilege due to their non-heterosexual, non-monosexual identity, but the experiences of a white, able-bodied, cisgender bisexual man will likely be quite different to those of a disabled, bi+ non-binary Person of Colour. While both people may battle with biphobia, the latter also may have to contend with ableism, transphobia and racism as well.

What's more, discrimination can overlap. Bi+ People of Colour don't just face biphobia and racism separately; they will likely experience a specific cross-section of the two. Biphobia and misogyny don't exist in isolation, but merge to create bimisogyny, a distinctive form of oppression reserved for bi+ women. Depending on your gender, race, ability, class, level of education, body size, and so on, you may experience more layers of oppression than other bi+ people. Everything from your culture to your daily experiences may differ from those of bi+ people with different backgrounds.

In this chapter, we're going to dive further into some of the unique challenges that may be faced by bi+ people from different backgrounds – in particular, bi+ women, men, trans and non-binary people, People of Colour and disabled people.

Now, some of these identities are not my own – as a white woman, I cannot speak on behalf of men, for example, or People of Colour. Instead, in this chapter, I'm platforming the voices of the people who hold these identities. You'll hear from me in the first section, on bi+ women and bimisogyny, but then I'll hand over to some other people who have lived experience and professional expertise in each of these areas.

Lewis Oakley will explore the topic of bisexual men and masculinity as, while men themselves aren't considered a marginalized group, bi+ men are definitely underrepresented. Mark Cusack, in his section, discusses the nuance of being bi+ and trans, and having an identity that is fluid in both gender and orientation. AFLO details the long-standing impact that colonialism has had on bi+ People of Colour, and Eliza Rain talks about navigating life, physically and mentally, as a bi+ disabled person.

While I'm eternally grateful to these talented people for lending their voices to my book, it's important to note that they don't speak on behalf of all bi+ people from these marginalized communities. For example, one bisexual disabled person will not have the exact same experiences as another. So when you read these pieces, keep in mind that they are representative of some, but not all, multiply marginalized bi+ people.

This chapter might be tough reading, especially if you relate to any of these specific discriminatory experiences, and I encourage you to practise self-care and take breaks if you need to. But when we fight against oppression, it's essential that we don't default to talking about the most privileged bisexual identities. The bi+ community is vast, nuanced and diverse, so our conversations about biphobia must be too.

Bi+ women: Not for you

Laura Clarke (she/they), sex educator and author

On a London bus in May 2019, Christine Hannigan and Melania Geymonat Ramirez were attacked by a group of young men. Upon realizing that the women were on a date, the men asked them to kiss and began making lewd sexual gestures, saying that they 'wanted to be shown how lesbians have sex'.[2] When the women declined, the aggression escalated from verbal to physical – suddenly they were surrounded, pelted with coins and punched in the face so hard that Christine was left with a broken jaw and Melania with a broken nose. A photo of the two women was quickly circulated on the internet, blood staining their faces and shirts, and the news soon reported that a 'lesbian couple' had been attacked.

A month later, in a piece for *The Guardian*, Christine bravely took back power and recounted her own version of that terrifying night. She told the world that she was, in fact, bisexual (hello, bi erasure!) and sought to 'highlight the misogyny embedded in the violence'.[3]

'Bimisogyny' describes the intersection of biphobia and misogyny, typically experienced by women, and people who are incorrectly perceived to be women (such as some non-binary people and trans men).

I'm yet to meet a bi+ woman who hasn't been subjected to

some type of bimisogyny, and fetishization in particular is an experience shared by many. To fetishize somebody is to view or treat them as a sexual object, instead of a human being with their own desires and opinions. For example, have you ever heard someone say 'I'd tap that'? (The 'that' being a living, breathing woman, not a contactless credit card.)

For bi+ women, it's not uncommon to hear 'Can I watch?', 'Threesome?' or 'That's hot' on coming out to a man. And while both lesbian and bisexual women experience these sexist remarks, more men fancy their chances of a threesome with a bi woman, because they believe she not only fancies the other woman, but him as well.

When I've come out to boyfriends in the past, I've feared being seen as an opportunity for them to live out their woman-on-woman fantasies. It's as if my sexuality suddenly belongs to them instead of me.

Fetishization is misleading – it makes it seem as if bi women experience more approval of their sexualities than most LGBTQIA+ people. While other queer people are tolerated at best, bi women are celebrated by men. But, as Shiri Eisner addresses in *Bi: Notes for a Bisexual Revolution*, acceptance is not without conditions: 'Rather than accepted, female bisexuality is "encouraged" on the sole grounds that it be palatable to straight men.'[4]

Much of this fetishization comes from the media. While

bi+ women are undeniably afforded the most visibility on our screens (compared to bi+ men and non-binary people), this often comes at the cost of our own agency. Bi women are represented through the 'male gaze' – a term coined by Laura Mulvey to describe how the media portrays women in a way that prioritizes the enjoyment of straight men – typically as sexual objects.[5]

Mainstream 'lesbian' porn (pornography depicting women having sex with other women, regardless of the sexual orientation of the people involved) is a prime example of the male gaze – how many women in real life only have sex in full glam makeup and stilettos? Let's be real, bed sheets are too expensive to stain with mascara and rip with dagger-sharp heels.

The fetishization of bi+ women, along with the myth that bi people are always up for sex, makes people (often men) feel entitled to our bodies, and this bimisogyny can turn violent. Christine and Melania's story on the bus is sadly just one example of many. Studies show that bisexual women are more likely to experience sexual violence (not including rape) than heterosexual women, lesbians or bi men (75% of bi women, compared to 43% of straight women, 46% of lesbians and 47% of bi men).[6]

Additionally, if you're a bi woman, you're more than three times more likely to be raped (61%) than a straight woman (17%), and almost five times more likely than a lesbian (13%).

The numbers for bi men were too small to reliably estimate in this study.[7]

Sexual violence isn't the only issue in which bi+ women are affected in greater numbers. Bisexual women are also more likely to live in poverty,[8] have a higher risk of substance abuse[9] and are more likely to be living with mental illness.[10] When comparing these horrifying statistics to the experiences of women with other sexual orientations (straight and lesbian), and to those of bi men, it becomes clear that this isn't solely an issue of misogyny, or of biphobia, but a unique blend of the two.

It's highly likely that worse health and social outcomes for bi+ women are the direct result of bimisogyny and minority stress. Would you feel happy to go to a doctor who repeatedly, and incorrectly, assumed your sexuality? If you'd experienced sexual violence, would your mental health go unscathed? How might your ability to work and make money be impacted if your mental health was suffering so badly that even getting out of bed felt impossible?

At this point, you might be cursing the straight population for the endless discrimination that bi+ women face, and the impact it has on our health and wellbeing. (Go ahead and scream into a pillow if you like. I'll wait.) But while a lot of this mistreatment comes from heterosexual people, they are not the only perpetrators of bimisogyny.

As we saw in Chapter Six, many monosexual gay and lesbian people have biphobic beliefs and contribute to the discrimination that bi+ people experience. And evidence shows that bisexual women encounter this the most – 27% of bi women report experiencing discrimination from others in the LGBTQIA+ community (compared to 18% of bi men, 9% of lesbians and 4% of gay men).[11]

Studies have shown that lesbians in particular are reluctant to date bisexual women,[12] often due to the perception that bi women are a flight risk – that they will eventually end up cheating with, or leaving their partner for, a man. And while some gay men refuse to date bi men, this issue doesn't impact the bi male community in quite the same way:

> Lesbian women view bisexual women as being more sexually attracted to men than to women, which in turn makes them dislike bisexual women. Gay men, on the other hand, have fewer reasons to dislike bisexual men since bisexual men's orientation is perceived to lean in a same-gender direction.[13]

Hmm, I wonder what this is called… If you said 'phallocentrism', you get a gold star.

Bisexuality in women seems to be the most palatable type of queerness to many heterosexuals, but bi+ women are often viewed the most negatively by other queer people.

Coincidence? I think not. Both of these issues seem to stem from the (incorrect) assumption that bi women are 'basically straight' – making us allies to straight people, but traitors to other queers.

More work needs to be done to combat bimisogyny across all communities and it starts with us calling out the problem. If you're a bi+ woman or girl, and reading this section has left you feeling helpless, remember that you're not. If you didn't already, you now know what bimisogyny is, and knowledge is power. Use your voice to advocate for change, report all sexual harassment, no matter how 'minor', and kiss girls because *you* want to, not to impress boys (not even really, really cute ones).

Bi+ men: A vicious cycle

Lewis Oakley (he/him), bisexual activist

Given the work I do in the bisexuality space, I have the privilege of meeting many bi+ people, both virtually and in person. They often have questions, but one illustrates the issues facing bi+ men more than any other. On the subject of coming out, one young man once asked me: 'If most women aren't open to dating bisexual men, isn't coming out as bi just coming out as gay by default?'

This question encapsulates so much about the intersection of bisexuality and masculinity.

One of the biggest challenges bisexual men face is the stigma that they are, in fact, closeted gay men. This assumption says more about societal attitudes than it does about the men themselves. There is a deep belief that a man's attraction to men overrides any attraction he might have to women. If a man has had sex with men, society struggles to believe that he could find women equally attractive.

A factor that intensifies this issue is that many gay men identify as bisexual on their way out of the closet. This creates a damaging stigma that all bisexual men are doing the same thing – destined to eventually come out as gay. Examples in popular culture, and often in people's personal experience, reinforce this belief, leaving bisexual men caught in a web of misconceptions.

This feeds directly into the reluctance many women have to date bisexual men. A 2016 Glamour survey revealed that 63% of women wouldn't date a man who'd had sex with another man, regardless of his sexual identity.[14] Similarly, a 2019 YouGov poll found that only 28% of women would be comfortable with a bisexual partner.[15] When looking for reasons for this, a study in the *Journal of Bisexuality* showed that straight women perceive bi men as less romantically and sexually attractive than straight men.[16]

The research tracks with what I've experienced first-hand, and the experiences that other bi men have shared with me.

Many women fear that a bi partner could eventually leave them for a man, or that they alone might not be able to satisfy all his needs. Some also believe that bi men are more promiscuous or incapable of monogamy.

In my experience, there is also an undercurrent of masculinity expectations here. Many women seek a partner who embodies traditional masculinity, part of which is often assumed to be an exclusive attraction to women. A man's attraction to both sexes is seen by some as a diminishment of his masculinity, reducing his desirability.

The knowledge that coming out as bi will be a turn off for many of the people they are attracted to often leads to bisexual men staying in the closet. Bisexual men are among the most closeted within the entire LGBTQIA+ community. According to a report by Stonewall, just 36% of bi individuals are out to their friends and only 20% to their families, compared to 74% and 63% respectively in the gay and lesbian population.[17]

When broken down by gender, a study by PEW Research found that just 12% of bi men were out of the closet.[18] The truth is, a significant percentage of bisexual men choose not to come out, knowing that it could harm their chances of forming relationships with women.

The reluctance to come out is further compounded by discrimination bi+ men often face from within the

LGBTQIA+ community. A report by Taimi in 2023 found that just 2% of bisexual men believe they are perceived positively by the LGBTQIA+ community.[19] With statistics like this in mind, it's understandable that for many bi men, it feels easier to stay on the down-low rather than being out, proud, and true to who they are.

This is all part of a vicious cycle. The fewer bisexual men who come out, the fewer role models there are for others to look to for advice or inspiration. We lack examples of openly bisexual men in successful, and, more importantly, happy relationships. Such examples are scarce in the media and even rarer in our personal lives.

This contributes to a sense of isolation, which I believe is one of the biggest challenges we face. It means bisexuality remains stagnant, never truly evolving, because so few people are willing to take the risk of coming out, being brave and setting an example.

It's also important to recognize that these issues compound and contribute to mental health challenges for bi+ men. When a person's identity is invalidated or misrepresented, it can exacerbate existing struggles with self-acceptance and belonging, making bi+ men feel caught between two worlds that don't fully recognize them.

The constant pressure to fit into narrow categories of sexual orientation can lead to internalized stigma, which is known to negatively impact mental wellbeing. Without easily available support networks, many bi men may feel alone in their experiences, compounding the emotional toll of living in a society that frequently erases their identities.

I am hopeful, however, that the tide is turning. As awareness grows and more bisexual men declare themselves publicly and proudly, the stigma will start to erode. As more bisexual people come out, society will begin to challenge the preconceived notion that we are just gay men in hiding. As that perception is shattered, more women might become comfortable with the idea of having a bisexual partner, without feeling any embarrassment or shame. This could encourage others to take that chance as well.

Additionally, as vocal bisexual individuals challenge the negative attitudes within the LGBTQIA+ community and push for better representation, we might see more organizations putting effort, time and, importantly, funding into improving the lives and lived experiences of bisexual men everywhere.

But this won't happen without effort and focus. Bi+ men have so far been neglected by society and the LGBTQIA+ community – and that needs to change. The issues facing bi men are glaringly obvious, not shrouded in mystery in the slightest. It truly would not take much effort to improve the world for all bi+ men.

Bi+ trans and non-binary people: Breaking boundaries

Mark Cusack (he/they), author, educator and coach

Being bi+ is about having a broad, expansive view of the genders you feel attracted to – it naturally follows that many of us perceive gender itself as equally expansive. Sexuality is about the gender(s) a person is attracted to, while gender identity reflects the gender(s) a person identifies with. In this light, sexuality and gender identity are intertwined; they can influence and inform one another.

It's entirely natural for someone to identify as both bi+ and trans or non-binary. These identities can coexist harmoniously, allowing people to navigate their attractions and sense of self without contradiction. Many don't realize that bi+ is the most common sexual orientation among trans and non-binary individuals[20] – when you perceive gender as a spectrum, it makes perfect sense that sexuality would be seen in a similarly diverse light.

Both bisexuality and gender diversity are frequently misunderstood. Many people hold ignorant assumptions about what these terms mean and how they intersect. Culturally, we are conditioned to view sexuality and gender identity through a binary lens. This narrow perspective leads to oversimplifications – like defining bisexuality merely as 'liking men and women' or perceiving a trans identity as simply 'a man becoming a woman' or vice versa. People may also dismiss our identities as a trend associated only with younger generations. These assumptions misrepresent the richness and diversity of our real lived experiences.

Then comes the relentless barrage of probing and inappropriate questions. These can range from demands for 'evidence' that bisexuality or gender diversity 'exists', to intrusive inquiries about the biology or psychology underpinning our identities. People may ask how we can be 'sure' of our identities or whether it might simply be a 'phase'. The burden of these questions can be emotionally draining, especially for those of us who hold more than one marginalized identity.

Society often portrays our identities as odd or different, placing the onus on us to educate those around us. We might feel pressure to 'soften' one part of ourselves to simplify things for others. We may have questions of our own about how the cis-heteronormative world works; however, we are just assumed to know this already, because we are queer. We may also have questions about our own identities and rarely have access to the information or role models to help us through our questioning.

Sometimes inappropriate questions and assumptions can lead to sexual harassment or abuse. Both bisexual and trans/non-binary identities can be highly fetishized. People may think that we are promiscuous or sexually open. They may find us 'exciting' or 'novel' and expect things from us that we are not comfortable with. Bi+ and trans/non-binary people have some of the highest rates of sexual trauma of any demographic, so it is important to take good care of ourselves and reach out if we need support.

People with marginalized identities are frequently viewed through a single lens. Prejudice thrives on categorizing individuals into rigid boxes, allowing for simplified judgements to be made. Consequently, those of us who embody multiple, intersecting identities often find ourselves reduced to just one aspect of who we are.

Common comments may look like: 'You can love who you want, but this trans thing is a step too far' or, 'What will it be next? This is so confusing!' People with diverse identities are often made to feel that one queer identity is acceptable but possessing two is 'too much'.

The trans community faces hostility in many parts of the world. As a result, a bisexual trans person might primarily be perceived as trans, because that is the trait that people find the most 'different' or 'controversial'. This reductive view neglects their bisexuality, contributing to bi erasure.

Sadly, bi+ and trans/non-binary people may share the experience of being viewed as undesirable. Stereotypes portraying us as 'indecisive' or 'untrustworthy' can create barriers to dating. Partners might feel insecure, fearing that we may be attracted to someone else or questioning whether they are 'enough' to satisfy the different aspects of our identities.

Sometimes, bi+ trans/non-binary individuals may come out to their partners during a relationship. While some partners respond well, others may struggle to accept it and feel as if they have been somehow betrayed or lied to. This can be immensely challenging for those of us who simply want to share our true selves with the ones we love.

Negative stereotypes can lead to bi+ trans/non-binary individuals feeling guilty in relationships. We may perceive our identities as burdensome to our partners or feel undesirable for not fitting the 'norm'. This internal conflict can result in tension, breakups, or even abusive dynamics. When challenges arise in a relationship, the blame is often placed on us for being 'different' or 'difficult'.

One of the most painful experiences for bi+ trans/non-binary individuals can be facing discrimination from within the LGBTQIA+ community itself. We can often receive hurtful or ignorant comments or simply be made to feel out of place in a community which is, in many places, still dominated by cis-gay people and stereotypes.

Bi+ trans and non-binary people frequently struggle to find opportunities and representation within the community. Many feel compelled to carve out their own spaces in order to find safety and acceptance, which can be a challenging but also (often) a creative and rewarding experience.

Despite the challenges, there is growing awareness that sexuality and gender are not always strictly defined categories. More people are identifying somewhere along the spectrum. Being bi+ and trans or non-binary is a wonderful way to be. It embodies an openness and broadness that can be incredibly liberating.

It's important to remember that you are valid exactly as you are, even if other people don't 'get it'. You don't owe anyone an explanation of your identity, and you shouldn't feel pressured to fit into boxes that don't represent you. Celebrating your diverse identity can enrich not only your life but also the lives of those around you. Embracing all your intersecting identities can be hard, but know that you are not alone.

Bi+ people of colour: Bi-passing colonial legacies

AFLO, the poet (she/they), spoken word artist, activist and academic

Being bi+ and belonging to the Global Majority – a collective term for people of Indigenous, African, Asian or Latin American descent, who make up approximately 85% of the global population[21] – can be a tricky position to navigate. This intersection can feel particularly lonely, and bi+ People of Colour can feel as if they are at a crossroads with the apparent need to 'choose' between their sexuality or their ethnic heritage.

Bi+ People of Colour face discrimination and exclusion in multiple spaces, and may face rejection or pressure to conform to heteronormative standards from their families, who may view bisexuality as a deviation from religious and cultural norms. Religious beliefs contribute to unfavourable opinions of queer people, which can lead to the exclusion of bi+ people from religious communities, as well as causing internal conflict for bi+ people themselves.

Traditional views on sexuality informed by religious and cultural norms can cause conflict within families, resulting in emotional distress or even estrangement. This pressure to conform to cultural norms can force bi+ People of Colour to hide their sexuality or suppress their identity. This rejection by their family can cause emotional distress and a sense of isolation, having a detrimental impact on their mental health and wellbeing.

But the stigma and rejection facing bi+ People of Colour hasn't always been this way. Colonialism – when one country takes control of another, exploiting resources and communities of people – has had a huge impact on understandings of sexuality around the world. The British Empire, from the late 16th to the early 20th century, was one of the largest colonial powers, controlling many countries across Africa, Asia and the Americas.

In many pre-colonial societies, people had diverse views on sexuality, including bisexuality, but British colonial powers forced binary understandings of gender and heteronormative frameworks of sexuality on the people they colonized.[22] The colonizers believed strongly in Christianity, and they imposed their Christian beliefs on colonized societies, disrupting indigenous ways of understanding gender and sexuality. Colonial rulers saw their own culture as superior and sought to replace or suppress the local cultures and practices, including more accepting views on sexuality.

Through the Empire, the British introduced laws across the globe that enforced strict ideas about sexuality, criminalizing behaviours that didn't fit their heteronormative views.[23] This led to the erasure of many beliefs and practices of indigenous people that existed before colonial rule, including their inclusive attitudes towards sexuality.[24]

Due to this erasure of history, bi+ People of Colour continue to face stigma and rejection from Communities of Colour to this day. But, if we could learn more about how bi+ people not only existed but were actually accepted before colonialism, maybe we could change that.

Sexuality is closely linked to gender, and indigenous understandings of gender can teach us a lot about the fluidity often associated with pre-colonial ideas around sexuality. For example, many First Nations cultures in North America (or Turtle Island) recognized 'Two-Spirit' identities, a term that encompasses a range of gender and sexual diversity.[25] Two-Spirit people could embody both masculine and feminine traits and could have relationships with people of any gender, reflecting a broader, more fluid understanding of sexuality and gender.[26] Among the Lakota Sioux, Two-Spirit individuals were integral in their communities, often seen as having a unique spiritual role and respected as healers, mediators and ritual leaders.[27]

Similarly, in pre-colonial India and South Asian cultures, Hijras were recognized as a 'third gender', and they often held ceremonial and ritualistic roles.[28] The existence of Hijras was woven into the social fabric of the times. Additionally, texts such as the *Kama Sutra* were an important part of this society.[29] The *Kama Sutra*, which is believed to have been written between 400 and 300 BCE, talks about the existence of diverse sexual orientations and practices, including bisexuality.[30]

In pre-Columbian South America, particularly within the Inca Empire, diverse sexualities were also recognized and accepted.[31] The Inca society acknowledged the existence of same-sex relationships and individuals who did not conform to traditional gender roles. In some regions, such as among the Quechua people, there were rituals and roles for people who engaged in relationships with both genders, often linked to spiritual or shamanistic practices.[32]

Similarly, in pre-colonial Māori society, there was recognition of same-sex relationships under the term 'takatāpui'.[33] Research shows that prior to colonialism and the introduction of Christianity, Māori communities actively accepted and embraced sexual diversity, as well as gender diversity.[34]

In pre-colonial Africa, numerous societies recognized bi+ and fluid sexualities. For example, among the Yoruba people of Nigeria, the concept of 'ase', a spiritual power, allowed individuals to transcend traditional gender roles, and same-sex relationships were not uncommon or stigmatized. The Yoruba religion includes deities and spirits that transcend traditional gender binaries, which reflects a more flexible view of sexuality within this traditional belief system.[35]

In Akan societies in Ghana and West Africa, there were documented cases of fluid sexual relationships.[36] Although Akan societies were predominantly heterosexual, some historical accounts suggest that same-sex relationships, including bisexual interactions, were not uncommon.[37]

The Dogon people of Mali are another example of an African community with complex understandings of gender and sexuality.[38] Traditional Dogon cosmology includes multiple deities and spiritual beings that do not adhere strictly to male or female categories.[39] This flexible understanding of gender is reflected in their social structures and rituals, which can encompass various forms of sexual and romantic relationships, including bisexuality.[40]

Additionally, the Buganda kingdom in Uganda had roles such as the 'Banja' who were culturally recognized for their same-sex relationships and unique gender expressions.[41]

From these multiple examples, we can see a pattern – before the influence of colonialism, various indigenous cultures recognized and integrated diverse sexualities, including bisexuality, into their societies and spiritual understandings. There is clearly a rich tapestry of sexual and gender diversity that existed in various indigenous communities prior to the existence of the British Empire. Therefore, the stigma faced by bi+ people in Global Majority communities is not a true reflection of those cultures – it is just another harmful legacy of colonialism.

The rejection of the heteronormativity and gender binaries by People of Colour is a return to our roots – we are returning to the way things were supposed to be. Thankfully, many of us are realizing this, and I myself have found so much validation, strength and love from other bi+ People of Colour who are unlearning colonialism and its teachings.

Unfortunately, some folks and elders within our communities do not know the richness of their histories, and this is yet another harmful colonial legacy. Instead, what we can do as bi+ People of Colour is continue to talk about and share our pre-colonial histories. Bisexuality existed long before the British Empire began its exploits, and we will continue to exist loudly in our many, many forms.

Bi+ disabled people: Doubly invisible

Eliza Rain (they/them), disabled content creator

I am an ambulatory wheelchair user – this, for me, means I use a wheelchair for long distances of walking, but I am able to walk and stand for short periods of time. 'Long distances' is an odd measurement, and is personal to the individual – for some people long distance means six miles, while for others it means a few metres. I personally haven't left the house without my wheelchair for around four years.

I am also bisexual – something I've known about myself since primary school. I remember having a crush on a girl in my class, but struggling to understand what this meant. This was because, at the time, most of the media I had seen only depicted people who were straight. I remember questioning how it could be possible to like someone who isn't a man, while being sure that I liked boys too. I brought this to my parents, who explained to me what it means to be bisexual and, as time went on, I realized that this was the right label for me.

Although I haven't always used a wheelchair, I have experienced issues my entire life that have made me struggle. Throughout my time at school, I would often be taken out of class and put into separate learning groups, as I wasn't able to 'keep up' with other children my age. Because of this, I would frequently miss out on various different types of education, which is very common for disabled people. In my case, I was often excluded from sex education.

I grew up in the 90s/00s, and honestly, the sex education wasn't great anyway – at no point did I learn about different sexualities. I wasn't taught about being LGBTQIA+ at all – in addition to being disabled, I also attended a Christian school where even the LGBTQIA+ members of staff were told to hide their sexuality.

Unfortunately within our society, disabled people are often seen as 'non-sexual' beings and are, as a result, left out of vital sex education lessons that allow them to have a better understanding of how to have safe sex, how to better understand their own sexuality, and how to explore it safely.

As a disabled bisexual person, this is a bit of an odd space to be in – disabled people are wrongly seen as inherently 'non-sexual', while bi+ people are (incorrectly) stereotyped as 'hypersexual' or 'more likely to cheat'. As a disabled bisexual person this means I sit at a weird cross-section of both stereotypes. People often think that I'll just date one person and settle down, or automatically assume I'm straight, because how could I be anything else? Additionally, anyone I do date is, of course, a *hero* for going out with a disabled person. (Huge eye roll!)

In relationships, I am seen as a burden because I am disabled – people often see me as a 'pointless' part of the relationship because I can't 'give as much', which, again, isn't true! Just because someone is disabled, it doesn't mean that we are any 'less' in a relationship or don't contribute as much – we are just as important members of the relationship as those who are not disabled.

When you are a disabled bisexual person, it can be even harder to find romantic or sexual relationships – unfortunately, some people are 'put off' by the idea of a disabled partner. The addition of bisexuality means that straight people might not go out with us as we aren't 'straight enough' but LGBTQIA+ people may not date us because we aren't 'queer enough'. Of course, these concepts are made up, and being bisexual is valid in and of itself. However, people have nasty misconceptions about both disabled and bi+ people, which can be doubly harmful to people who hold both of these identities.

It can also be much harder to meet people when you are a bisexual disabled person as many LGBTQIA+ spaces aren't wheelchair accessible. LGBTQIA+ spaces have a long history of needing to be hidden away for safety and, as a result, are often in basements or areas that are harder to access. Many haven't been updated to be wheelchair accessible due to funding, meaning that lots of LGBTQIA+ spaces are completely inaccessible to wheelchair users.

Existing as a bi+ disabled person isn't always easy, but there are many of us out there – a study published by Stonewall in 2020 found that 44% of bi people identified as disabled.[42] And what's more, organizations are increasingly recognizing our community and our needs. For example, ParaPride – an empowerment charity that advocates for the visibility, education and awareness of LGBTQ+ disabled people:

> ParaPride started on the basis of a need to address the lack of inclusion for Disabled people within the LGBTQ+ community; a need for more accessible LGBTQ+ spaces; and a need to promote body positivity around different bodies and being able to celebrate that.[43]

A wonderful community is out there, filled with love and joy and understanding – it might just take us a little longer to find it.

I hope this chapter has added some more context to biphobic discrimination, and the specific ways it can affect different bi+ people. If you do identify with any of the experiences within this section, it might be distressing to acknowledge the additional hurdles you may face because of particular aspects of your identity.

But whether you share these experiences or not, they are relevant to you as a bi+ person. We all have a responsibility to be diverse in our activism, to raise the voices of underrepresented and underprivileged queer people, to recognize that, when we come out as bi+ people, we don't all do so from the same starting line.

Step Bi Step...

- Intersectionality refers to the unique forms of discrimination experienced by people with multiple marginalized identities.
- Not all bi+ people will share the same experiences of biphobia – our gender, race, ability, culture, religion, body size, and so on might inform the oppression we face.
- When we fight against biphobic oppression, it's vital that we do not just do so through a white, cisgender, able-bodied lens. We must uplift the voices that are frequently forgotten, and strive for equality for *all* bi+ people.

Chapter Eight

Coming Out

So, you know you're bi+ and that the world might have opinions about it. What's next?

Coming out (a shortened version of 'coming out of the closet') is a metaphor used to describe the process of LGBTQIA+ people telling others about their sexual orientation or gender identity. Some people begin the coming out process while still in the midst of figuring out their identity – this was my experience with my closest friends. They might say something like, 'I think I'm bi' or, 'I'm questioning my identity' or, 'I actually feel more like a girl than a boy'. However, lots of queer people like to do the self-discovery process alone, and only come out to others when they're 100% sure.

But why is coming out specifically a queer thing? Why are LGBTQIA+ people the only ones expected to formally declare their sexuality or gender identity? The fact is, we live in a world where everyone is assumed to be heterosexual and cisgender until proven otherwise. People think of straight, cisgender people as the default factory setting for humans, while being queer is either a bonus feature or a bug, depending on who you ask. The assumption that everyone is straight is called heteronormativity and the expectation that everyone will identify with the gender they were assigned at birth is called cisnormativity.

Most people don't like feeling misunderstood. Coming out can be a way to share the most authentic parts of ourselves with our loved ones – to live openly and freely as who we really are. It's a way of saying, 'Here I am and I'm proud.'

> There is a power and a joy in living in the light, authentically and openly. I take great pleasure in knowing that – by living my own life in public – I am serving as a beacon and as a possibility model to others. I also really love being a part of the bi+ global community. I like being around people committed to thinking beyond binaries, people who have the integrity and courage to live life outside of conventional norms. (ROBYN OCHS (SHE/THEY), SPEAKER, EDUCATOR, WRITER AND EDITOR OF *BI WOMEN QUARTERLY*)

That's the wholesome version. But, if we're being cynical, coming out also panders to a hetero- and cisnormative society and feeds the machine that oppresses us. We mark ourselves as 'different', and by doing so we reiterate the divide between cishet and queer people. (Heavy, right?)

Now, I'm not saying that coming out is inherently harmful. You're not going to be cancelled for sitting your mum down and telling her you're bi. But what it *does* mean is that you don't owe anyone a coming out. It is not your responsibility to set the record straight (or rather, queer) with family members, to share parts of yourself that feel private, or to make a big emotional declaration in order to live the life you want to live. If you're a closeted queer (someone who hasn't yet come out) then you're still queer. Coming out isn't the last step in being awarded your bi+ stripes; you've already earned them by being your wonderful self.

Another common misconception about coming out is that it's a one-time thing – 'Mum, Dad, I'm bisexual' and a big sigh of relief. But what about your friends? Your teachers? Boyfriends, girlfriends, partners? Your uncle? The person making your future wedding cake? It's simply not possible to tell everybody in the world that you're bi+ all in one go.

> Being bi is exhausting because you have to constantly come out to every new person you get close to, in order for them to truly understand you. (JESSE (HE/HIM), AGE 17)

I first came out when I was 12. Now, in my late twenties, I still come out regularly. For example, I was at the gym with my personal trainer and she asked who my celebrity crushes were: 'David Tennant and Gillian Anderson.' 'Wait, you're bi?' 'Yep!'

Fortunately, most of my experiences of coming out have gone quite smoothly. As society becomes more familiar with and accepting of queer identities, it's increasingly likely that our families and friends will accept us for exactly who we are. But this doesn't necessarily make coming out any less nerve-wracking, even if we're 99% sure that we'll get a positive response.

> I first properly realized I was queer in my early twenties. I think it was the first time I gave myself permission to see myself outside the very heteronormative lens I'd grown up in. It wasn't that

> queerness was shunned or disregarded when I was growing up – my family were lefty and I remember my mum taking me to the London Pride parade as a kid. But it was all viewed very much from the perspective of an ally, and it took a while to realize all the things I'd felt throughout my life (not quite fitting in, finding my relationships with straight men kind of strange, and the biggie: having massive crushes on women) weren't things that everyone experiences. Once I came out and began reflecting on my childhood and teenage years, it was so obvious this was who I'd always been. (RUBY RARE (SHE/THEY), AUTHOR OF *SEX ED: A GUIDE FOR ADULTS* AND *THE NON-MONOGAMY PLAYBOOK*)

Coming out – to yourself and to other people – takes time. It is ongoing. For many, many bi+ people, coming out can be an affirming experience – friends and family who are instantly supportive, scooping you up and telling you they love you no matter what. But sometimes, leaving the closet doesn't feel quite so celebratory. You might face dismissive remarks, awkward conversations or even dangerous situations.

However, if you're thinking of telling people that you're bi, there's plenty you can do to make it go as smoothly as possible. If I could hold your hand while you share the news, I would. But I can't. So instead, here is a guide all about how to come out – a metaphorical bi big sister hand-squeeze.

How to come out

Perfect timing

Timing can make such a difference in the response that you get from your loved ones. Try to avoid coming out when you know someone is in a bad mood, or is mad at you for another reason. If you're in the middle of a blazing row with your dad, he might not be in the best place to hear what you have to say and respond in a way that makes you feel respected. Try to choose a time when people seem in good spirits.

That said, you might want to avoid coming out at Christmas, or on your family summer holiday. If things do go badly, you might end up feeling like a special occasion has been 'spoiled' (even though it wouldn't be your fault at all!).

And finally, make sure you give yourself and your loved one enough time to have a conversation if needed. They will probably be more receptive if they're not in the process of rushing out of the door for work, and they might like to have the time to ask questions or spend time with you afterwards. I would make sure that they have at least half an hour to spare. Remember that you've had lots more time to get your head around this than they have!

Start with a trusted person

Maybe you have people in your life that you're worried about telling. Maybe your grandparents have expressed negative views about LGBTQIA+ people in the past, or one of your friends has joked that bisexuals are 'greedy'.

But equally, there might be somebody who you count on as a safe person to tell – a friend who is bi+ themselves, or an aunt who is as big of a fan of *Heartstopper* as you. Congratulations, you've identified your Trusted Person.

You might want to come out to your Trusted Person before you tell anyone else. This way, you get the opportunity to practise what you're going to say, without being worried that you'll receive a biphobic response. It takes away the tension a little bit and prepares you to share the news with people you're less sure about.

Once you've told your Trusted Person, you might want to ask them to come with you when you tell other people. Maybe you bring your bestie when you tell your mum, or ask your dad to help you explain it to your grandparents. It can be nice to have backup if you're not sure how things will pan out (pun very much intended).

Location, location, location

Now you have your when and your who, it's time to think about where. Are you telling somebody in confidence? If so, you might want to make sure that you're somewhere that you can't be overheard. If you want to come out to your friends, it might be better to do it at their house after school instead of on the bus.

However, if you're worried about how somebody will react (especially if you don't feel safe with this person), coming out in a public place might be a less dangerous option. You might choose somewhere where there's lots of people around, but where you still have some privacy, like a park.

The absolute worst-case scenario when you come out is the other person getting violent – if you're worried about this, doing it in public might make them less likely to lash out, and there would be people around to help if things do turn nasty.

IRL or not?

Some people don't want to come out in person. Maybe they're nervous about the other person's reaction and they feel safer having some distance. Or perhaps they know they'll get emotional or flustered, and want to make sure that they express themselves properly.

Luckily, there are a number of tools at our disposal:

	Pros	Cons
Phone or video call	• You don't have to wait to see somebody in real life to come out. Helpful if you have relatives or friends who live far away! • You can hang up if the other person starts saying things that make you uncomfortable, upset or unsafe.	• Bad signal or internet could make the conversation patchy, which might be more difficult. • You can't guarantee that the other person is in a place where nobody else can overhear. • If you call somebody, you might catch them at a bad time. It can be harder to gauge their mood prior to the call.
Text or letter	• You can write and rewrite your coming out as many times as you want and get it perfect. You might find it easier to articulate yourself in writing, whereas in person you may get emotional or flustered. • You won't be interrupted! Doing a big speech in person is great but other people may chip in with questions or comments that throw you off.	• There is a possibility that your letter or text could be shown to other people. Once it's out there, you don't have control over who reads it. • Your words might be misinterpreted if people can't hear the tone behind them. People won't be able to ask clarifying questions in the moment and may be left feeling confused about certain things you've said.

	• You can send your text, or leave your letter somewhere, while being far away from the person you're coming out to. You might feel safer this way.	• You might feel anxious about not being able to see their initial reaction, or having to wait for their response. If they don't respond for a long time, how would you feel about this?
Social media post	• A great way to tell a lot of people at the same time! It can save you from having the same conversation over and over again. • Like a text or a letter, you can carefully articulate yourself in the caption and have the opportunity to share the news the way you feel is best. • You can post a cute picture of you with your Pride flag. Very aesthetic.	• If you're posting on social media, you really need to be okay with everyone in your life finding out – even your grandma who doesn't have Instagram. As with a text, someone could screenshot the post and show people who don't follow you. • People might be unkind in your comments section, or share the post to their page with a mean comment. (A good way to reduce this risk is by turning your comments off!) • Posting on social media can lack the personal touch. It might be a good way to come out to the people you know casually, but consider if you want your mum/dad/best friend to find out this way.

Once again, coming out isn't a one-time process – I'd recommend tailoring your approach depending on the person you're telling. Maybe coming out to your best friends in person sounds good, but you'd feel more comfortable telling your parents via a letter. There's no one-size-fits-all approach when it comes to breaking free of the closet!

> *For too long I didn't think being bi was 'important enough' to come out. I didn't think it was a big deal, probably because of the assumption that 'everyone is a little bisexual'. But actually coming out felt better than I could have ever imagined. You don't need a reason, or a relationship to come out – just do it if it's safe for you and it feels right. I can promise that you won't regret what it gives you: the ability to exist out loud as your true self.* (JEN WINSTON (SHE/THEY), AUTHOR OF *GREEDY: NOTES FROM A BISEXUAL WHO WANTS TOO MUCH*)

Give it time

While I truly hope that your coming out(s) goes well, and that you're instantly accepted for the brilliant person you are, sometimes people need a little more time to adjust.

Don't be surprised if people need a few hours/days/weeks to wrap their head around the fact that you're bi+. Some people will ask *a lot* of questions. Others might avoid you for a while. Some people might continue to mislabel you. This can be hard. You might feel as if you've bared your soul for nothing, or worse than nothing. But sometimes it just takes a while for somebody to realize that you're still the same person. You haven't changed, their perception has.

> *My advice to any queer person reading this is to be discerning about whose opinions you listen to. You have the right to explore who you are, who you desire, and who you love, and to have that evolve. Some people in our lives have really strong opinions about...honestly everything, and these folks usually have more opinions than expertise.* (DESIREE BURCH (SHE/HER), COMEDIAN AND PERFORMANCE ARTIST)

If you're made to feel uncomfortable, or there's a lot of tension at home, you might want to go and stay with your Trusted Person for a few days, or just call them to vent. In time, hopefully your loved one will adjust. But this might not come without some learning on their part.

Things to consider

In my experience, it's always better to hope for the best but prepare for the worst. Before you come out, there are a number of questions that you need to ask yourself to ensure your wellbeing and safety.

Why do I want to come out?

Is it because you want to be your authentic self with your family? Do you want to introduce your new boyfriend to your mates? Or is it because you feel pressure to? Take some time to think about what you're hoping to achieve from coming out. If you're not doing it for *you*, maybe reconsider if it's the right time.

Is this person trustworthy?

No matter who you tell, there is a chance that they will share this information with other people. If you're still in the closet with certain people in your life, consider if the person you're telling will keep your identity a secret if you ask them to.

How does this person feel about LGBTQIA+ people?

Some people will be very accepting (and maybe queer themselves!), while others will sadly hold harmful and upsetting views about bi+ people. And for certain people, you will have absolutely no idea how they're going to respond, because you've never talked about queerness with them before. You might want to test the waters with these people before you come out – you could say something like 'Did you see that [celebrity name] came out as bi?' or 'Oh wow, gay marriage was just legalized in [country].' Their response might inform whether or not you decide to tell them.

What policies does my school/ work have to protect me?

If you're coming out to people you go to school with or work with (including your teachers or employers), it might be a good idea to establish what policies your school or workplace have in place to protect you beforehand. Where do you go if you experience biphobic bullying? Is there an LGBT society you can attend? Does your company have a diversity network? Knowing your rights as a queer person is extremely valuable!

If this goes badly, will I be safe?

Probably most importantly, what is your plan to protect your mental and physical health if the person you're coming out to responds very negatively? Can you stay with your Trusted Person if you're kicked out of your home? Do you have enough money to get by if you're cut off financially? Do you have the phone number for an LGBT or mental health charity? (There are plenty in the Further Support section of this book.)

In many countries, like the UK and the USA, queer people are more privileged because our rights are protected by law. But in some countries, LGBTQIA+ people lack legal protections, and in others, being queer is illegal and can be punished by violence or death. If you live in a country where your rights are not protected, or your identity is criminalized, you will have to be even more sure that the person you're coming out to is somebody you can really trust.

> *I've come out to my friends, but I haven't to my parents. They come from a traditional Punjabi upbringing, and the cultural biases against queer people make me fear coming out.* (WREN (HE/HIM), AGE 17)

The talk

There are hundreds if not thousands of different responses that you might get when you come out. I couldn't possibly list them all, but here are some of the most common comments and scenarios and a few different options for how you might respond.

'Are you sure?'

This question may come from a place of genuine care about your choice to come out, or it might be a way of undermining what you've just said. Whether you're sure or not isn't important, what's important is that you're supported. So be honest.

- 'I know this is new for you, but I've had a long time to think and reflect and I'm confident that this is who I am.'
- 'I've actually known for a really long time and I waited to tell you until I was 100% sure.'

- 'No! I'm not sure. I'm still questioning a lot of things. But I wanted to tell you because I'm on the journey of figuring things out and I'd love your support while I do.'

'You're too young to know what you are!'

Ugghh. This one is very annoying and I'm sorry if this is the response you get. Unfortunately, being a teenager comes with a lot of being told you're not old enough to know things that you definitely already know. Stand your ground and be mature in your response, to show that you've given this proper thought.

- 'I know myself quite well. I know how I feel, and who I'm attracted to at this point in my life.'
- 'If I was heterosexual, you probably wouldn't say that I was too young to know that I'm straight.'
- 'Even if you think I'm going to change my mind in a few years, can you just support me in how I feel right now?'

'Why do you need to label yourself?'

As we mentioned at the start of the book, some people really don't like labels, and that's fine! But despite other people's preferences for themselves, your own labels should always be respected, so you might want to explain what a certain label means to you.

- 'I don't find labels restrictive, I find them empowering.'
- 'Labelling my identity as pansexual has allowed me to research and explore it in greater detail. I've found a community of people who share this label who have been a great help to me.'
- 'A label doesn't change who I am, or define every part of me. I'm still me, I'm just also bisexual.'

Lots of questions

People's questions often come from a genuine desire to learn and understand, but that doesn't make them any less exhausting to answer (especially if you've had the same conversation with everyone you've told!). You may want to shed more light on your identity, but you're also under no obligation to give a Bisexuality 101 lecture every time you come out.

- 'I'm happy to answer any questions you have. It's great that you want to learn more.'

- 'I don't mind answering a couple of your questions now, but then can we discuss it at a different time when I feel more able to respond?'
- 'I can answer some of your questions, but I'd love for you to do your own research too. There are some articles I can send you online, and there's also a book I'm reading that breaks down common myths and misconceptions about bi+ people. I can lend it to you.'

Negative response

A negative response is always hard. Depending on the situation, you might want to share how their words make you feel, challenge their views, or leave the situation entirely if it's unsafe or upsetting.

- 'I appreciate that this is a lot for you to take in, but what you're saying is really hurtful.'
- 'Have you heard something about bi+ people that makes you feel this way? There's a lot of misinformation out there; maybe we can talk about it.'
- 'I don't feel safe right now, so I'm stopping this conversation for today.'

Positive response

A positive response should be the bare minimum you receive, and you don't need to feel grateful just because somebody isn't biphobic. That said, you might also want to thank somebody if they've made you feel loved or accepted. I'm personally a fan of a big hug, but if that isn't your style, words can work just as nicely.

- 'Thank you so much, your words mean the world to me.'
- 'I'm so glad I get to be my authentic self with you now!'
- 'I knew you would be lovely about it but I was still a little nervous. Thanks for being amazing.'

> *I've come out to most of my friends and family and I've been lucky enough that they've been supportive. My favourite thing my family do is ask, 'So do you have a girlfriend?' and then quickly add 'or a boyfriend?'* (TOMMY (HE/HIM), AGE 14)

Being outed

Sometimes, unfortunately, somebody will take it upon themselves to reveal your identity to others without your consent. This is called being 'outed'. It shouldn't happen – your identity is yours to disclose and it's never okay to share private information about somebody's sexuality or gender identity.

When I was a teenager, I told a friend that I was bi+ and asked her to keep it a secret. She promised she would, and then told her mum. From then on, I felt uncomfortable whenever I was at her house. Her mum continued to be lovely to me, but I felt that she knew something private about me and I was terrified that she would tell my own parents, who didn't yet know. Worst of all, I felt as if my trust had been broken.

It's ultimately your decision if you decide to maintain a relationship with the person who outed you. Any emotions you have – anger, betrayal, fear – are valid and you have a right to tell the person how they've made you feel by breaking your trust. If you want to end the relationship, that's understandable. But if you decide to keep them in your lives, you might want to consider whether you continue to share private information with them.

If being outed has resulted in bullying or abuse from other people, including being made homeless by your family, then be sure to tell a trusted adult or contact one of the support services listed at the back of this book. There are people out there who will be able to help you navigate this difficult situation. You are not in this alone.

Step Bi Step...

- Only come out if *you* want to and you feel ready. You don't owe anybody access to private information about yourself, and coming out doesn't make you any more bi+.

- Coming out isn't a one-time thing – you will likely have to come out over and over again to different people, but it will get easier over time.

- There are lots of things to consider before you come out, including whether it's the right time and place, the words you want to say and, most importantly, how to prepare in case it goes badly. Hope for the best, prepare for the worst.

- If once you come out (or are outed) you are made to feel unsafe, or experience bullying or abuse, there are services you can reach out to at the back of this book.

Chapter Nine

Dating

When I was in my late teens, I went on my very first date with a girl. She was a friend – also bisexual – and it took a lot of courage to ask her out in the first place. It went really well – we talked, laughed and drank iced coffee with whipped cream. At the end of the date, just as I was about to lean in for a goodbye kiss, she turned to me and said, 'Okay, I've gotta run, I've got a date now with a guy I really like. Wish me luck!'

Yep. She thought I'd asked her out for coffee as a friend. She gushed some more about this new potential boyfriend before heading off towards town, leaving me feeling more than a little deflated.

While the dating world is complex at the best of times, dating when you're bi+ can often mean there's even more to consider. Romance is everywhere – from movies to reality TV to social media to mattress commercials – you'd think we'd know how it's done. Society has primed us for a heterosexual, monogamous relationship ever since we pressed 'play' on our first Disney movie. So when you start to date as a queer person, it can suddenly feel as if you've revised for the wrong exam.

Of course, not all bi+ people want romantic relationships, and that's fine! But if you're interested in dating, you might have the same questions as I did – where do I meet other queer people? What if my partner doesn't understand my bisexuality? How can my queerness flourish in a straight-presenting relationship?

This section breaks down all that and more – Dating 101 as a bi+ person.

How do I meet other queer people?

As a bi+ person, you're not limited to dating other LGBTQIA+ people – lots of bi and pan folks (including me) are in happy, respectful relationships with cishet people. But there are lots of reasons why you might specifically want to date other queer people:

- You have a preference for people of the same gender as yourself.

- You don't want to have to explain and justify your queer identity; you want someone who already gets it.
- You've never been in a relationship with another queer person and you want to try it!

Join a group

It seems as if the answer to meeting queer people is easy – gay bars! But if you're under the legal drinking age, this is probably a no-go. Luckily, there are more and more LGBTQIA+ youth groups and clubs popping up every day.

Joining one of these groups is a great idea for making friends, but they can also be a good place to find a boyfriend, girlfriend or partner. The people in these spaces will likely be around your age, and possibly from other schools – expanding your potential dating pool. LGBTQIA+ spaces are also just fantastic for meeting other people like you, and being able to exist loudly and proudly as your authentic queer self.

> *My favourite thing about being queer is the community and the vibrancy and diversity within it. Every time I go to queer events with my wife I feel like there's a magic there – that we all have a shared history and a fight within us that really brings us together.* (PEARL MACKIE (SHE/HER), ACTOR AND ACTIVIST)

Your town might not have an LGBT youth club specifically, but it might have a queer reading group, or running club, or yoga class. While there will definitely be more age diversity in these groups, you still might meet some people who are a similar age to you.

What's great about this option is that it allows you to hang out as friends first, giving you time to decide if you want to take things further. That way, you don't get the awkward moment on your first date where you realize that you have nothing in common and there's no spark!

These spaces are also one of the safest spots to meet people, as you'll likely have youth workers or club leaders running the space, and lots of other people around you in case something makes you feel uncomfortable.

Now unfortunately, while LGBTQIA+ people exist everywhere, it can be harder to find queer people your age if you live in a smaller town. Cities like London, New York and Los Angeles feel more liberal and queer-friendly than tiny, conservative villages in the middle of nowhere. Take it from someone who grew up in a seaside town in Wales and then moved to the queer haven of Brighton in my twenties – you really feel the difference. So what do you do if you feel as if you're the only bisexual in the village?

Go online

If you can't find a queer youth space IRL, the internet will have tons of them, from online LGBT groups run by charities, to teen dating apps, to huge queer Instagram communities. If trying to meet a young queer person in your area feels like trying to find a needle in a haystack, finding queers online is like finding a fork in the kitchen.

Obviously, when you're meeting people online, they could very feasibly be on the other side of the world. If that's the case, you need to decide if a long-distance relationship will work for you. With video chat, texts and social media, this works for a lot of people. (My partner and I were long-distance for a year of our relationship and, while we missed each other, it worked well!) Alternatively, you might find somebody who lives a 45-minute train ride away, and you can meet up with them at the weekend when you don't have school.

But here's the enormous, gigantic, important disclaimer that you were almost definitely expecting and are sick of hearing from adults: meeting up with people that you've connected with online can be *very dangerous.*

The internet is wonderful but it's also a place where people can hide who they really are. The person who you think is a 15-year-old student in a neighbouring school? That could be a 55-year-old man. Catfishing – when someone pretends to be someone they're not online – is very common and has resulted in people being assaulted or killed.

So, if you're talking to someone online, here are your golden rules:

- Don't send any personal or private information, including your address, school name, banking information, nudes or sexual messages. If you wouldn't post it on your public page, don't send it to a stranger.
- Don't meet up with someone without video-chatting with them first. Photos aren't good enough – it's all too easy to pass off another person's pictures as your own.
- Never, ever meet up with someone, especially for the first time, without bringing a friend. If you're worried that your friend will be a third wheel, tell the person you're meeting to bring a friend too and make it a double date or a group hang.
- Let someone know exactly where you're going, and what time you expect to be home. Check in with a

family member or friend via text to let them know that you're okay.

- Always meet up with someone in a public place – a cafe, a bowling alley, the town square – ideally in the daylight. Think, 'If I needed help, would someone be around to help me?'

I know this stuff has probably been drilled into you over and over in school and by your parents, but it's genuinely important. The internet can be an incredible place and open so many doors for queer people, but we should always exercise appropriate caution.

What do queer relationships look like?

Honestly? Whatever you want them to look like! You get to decide what type of relationship works best for you. There are two main styles of romantic relationship – monogamy and polyamory. Let's explore these in a little more detail, shall we?

Monogamy

Monogamy is when you and your partner date each other exclusively. This type of relationship is definitely considered more 'traditional' and there's a lot more representation of monogamous relationships in the media.

If you're bi+, a monogamous relationship could look like dating another queer person, or dating a straight person. You might decide that you only want to have relationships with other bi+ people, because you know that you're less likely to experience biphobia from a partner this way. That's a completely valid choice and you might see people talking about these types of relationships online using the hashtag #Bi4Bi.

Sometimes, bi+ people in monogamous relationships can feel as though their bisexual identity is being slowly erased. Not necessarily by their partner, but by society. If you're in a relationship with someone of a different gender, you might be assumed to be straight. And if you're with someone who is the same gender as you, people may assume that you're gay.

But your sexuality isn't defined by who you're dating. If you start to feel this way in a relationship, you should find some fun ways to honour your bi+ identity.

Here are some of the things you could do:

- Wear bi+ badges or iron-on patches on your jacket or backpack.
- Stick bi+ stickers on your laptop or water bottle.
- Hang a bi, pan or other multisexual flag on your bedroom wall.
- Go to bi-specific events, either with or without your partner.
- Celebrate bi-specific days like Bi Visibility Day on 23 September (a great excuse to bake a cake in the colours of your flag).
- Consume media depicting bi+ characters with your partner, and tell them the bits that feel authentic to your own experiences.
- Follow bi+ creators on social media and become part of a bi+ community online.

Equally, if you don't want to do any of this, and you go months or even years without outwardly acknowledging your bi+ identity, it doesn't make you any less bi.

Polyamory

Polyamory is when someone has romantic relationships with more than one person at a time. 'Wait, isn't that cheating?!' No! Because in polyamorous (polyam) relationships, everyone involved has consented to this dynamic. With cheating, someone is breaking an agreement that they'll be exclusive with another person.

In polyamory, each individual person can enter multiple relationships, but there are lots of different polyam dynamics. One person might have multiple partners who don't date each other, and they spend time with their different partners separately. Alternatively, sometimes their partners might be friends, or even date one another, creating more of a group dynamic.

While many bi+ people are fully satisfied with monogamy, others might feel that their bisexuality is erased in monogamous relationships, and that being polyamorous allows them to fully claim and experience their bisexuality, by having partners of different genders.

> My polyamory is an extension of my bisexuality. I feel I can fully express my bisexuality through non-monogamy. (LEANNE YAU (SHE/THEY), POLYAMORY EDUCATOR AND INFLUENCER)

As with monogamous relationships, boundaries are essential. Cheating is still possible in a polyamorous relationship. For example, you and your partner might decide to date other people, but agree that existing friends are off limits. If you then went on a date with your partner's bestie, that's breaking the mutual agreement you've made.

Polyamory can frighten some more traditionally minded people, because it defies societal norms, just like being queer does. The choice to date multiple people may be painted as greedy, or slutty, as bi+ people themselves are often stereotyped to be. But if polyamory is right for you, then you should embrace it. If you wouldn't let your sexuality be confined to a box, why should your relationship style be?

What makes a relationship healthy?

In any relationship – platonic or romantic, sexual or familial – respect, trust and autonomy are vital ingredients.

I've been in my fair share of unhealthy relationships – some of which I would now, in hindsight, describe as abusive. I am happy to report that I have also dated some truly wonderful people who have made me feel safe and supported. It's not arrogant to know your worth, and to recognize that you deserve love and respect of the highest possible quality.

So, here are some signs that you might be in a healthy relationship:

- You feel respected, listened to and supported.

- You feel safe from physical or emotional harm.
- Your partner doesn't try to pressure you into doing things you don't want to do (from watching a scary movie, to having sex).
- You feel loved by your partner for exactly who you are. You don't feel that they're trying to change you.
- Your partner respects your privacy. They don't feel entitled to you because you're in a relationship.
- You're able to spend time apart, and have your own hobbies and friends. You aren't entirely reliant on each other.
- You are able to resolve conflict without disrespecting one another (for example, shouting or insulting the other person). Arguments are often part of a healthy relationship – it's *how* you argue that's important.
- Your opinion matters just as much as your partner's.
- You feel like equals – there isn't a large imbalance of power.

Power imbalances occur in relationships all the time. Sometimes a power imbalance has the potential to be so great that laws are put in place to prevent relationships from happening between certain people – a teacher and a student, an adult and a minor. In situations like these, somebody is almost definitely being taken advantage of.

Some power imbalances are not against the law, and healthy relationships can occur even when one person has a slight advantage over the other in some way. Think about a couple where one partner has a well-paid job, while the other partner's job is staying at home, looking after the children. There is a financial imbalance of power here, but that doesn't necessarily mean that this relationship is unhealthy, or abusive.

You need to ask yourself if you feel like an equal in your relationship – would you still be able to stand up for yourself in an argument? Are you granted the same level of respect as your partner? Do you fear them, or feel that you need to tiptoe around them?

Historically, gender has played a huge role in who holds power in a heterosexual relationship. Women weren't allowed to work, own property or have their own bank accounts, and relied entirely on their husbands. While some people may still choose this life today, the difference is that this is typically now a *choice*.

But it's not all left in the past. Gender roles in heterosexual relationships persist to this day, and usually our social norms involve the man having the power – men pay for dinner, men make the first move, men open the car doors. The assumption is 'man' equals big, strong, rich, and 'woman' equals submissive, delicate, quiet.

In queer relationships, this dynamic may not exist. You might find yourself questioning how a relationship between two men or two women actually functions, as so much of what we're taught about relationships relies on men taking power and women giving it up.

> *Who walks down the aisle? Who proposes? Who pays for dinner? Who opens the door for the other? What if he's manlier than me?* (CHARLIE (HE/HIM), AGE 17)

But guess what? This is where you get to throw away the rulebook and create a relationship where you both exist on an equal footing. And ideally, even in relationships with someone of a different gender, you can continue to question and defy these gender norms. In my house, my husband does the cooking and I take out the bins – take that, patriarchy!

What makes a relationship unhealthy?

Of course, when somebody wields too much power, it can sometimes cause a relationship to become abusive. Spotting the signs of abuse is important – it's very easy to brush it off as you being overly sensitive, or them just having a bad day. But if your relationship exhibits any of the following signs, it could be time to re-evaluate if you're safe and happy:

- Your partner belittles you, mocks you or disrespects you.

- You don't feel able to be your true, authentic self.
- You feel as if your partner is always checking up on you, or violating your privacy (for example, checking your phone behind your back).
- You feel as if you have no breathing space – that you're being suffocated or are constantly having to walk on eggshells.
- Your partner pressures you to do things you don't want to do (for example, have sex or do drugs).
- Your partner isolates you from your friends or family, or wants you all to themselves.
- Your partner is physically abusive – hitting, shoving or hurting your body in some way – or is physically intimidating (for example, throwing things at or near you, shouting in your face).
- Your partner forces, pressures or manipulates you into being sexual with them, including forcing you to send nude photos or videos.
- Your partner disrespects or puts down aspects of your identity, including your race, gender or sexual orientation.

If you're bi+ and in a relationship with somebody who is straight or gay, you could experience biphobia from your partner, as I have in the past. This might take the form of an insensitive joke, something that you can talk about with your partner and resolve together. But it could be more serious, like somebody outing you, denying your identity or trying to convert you.

You might also experience homophobia or biphobia from other people if you're openly dating people of the same gender, from strangers to people in your personal life.

> *Dating as a queer teen is pretty terrifying. When I was 15, I had my first boyfriend, but all I can remember is how many people stared at us in public and how I couldn't even hug him when his parents were around. Around a year ago I went on a couple of dates with a girl I really liked, and when I casually brought up the fact I was bi, she left and told me she didn't want to see me any more.* (JESSE (HE/HIM), AGE 17)

If you do experience any type of abuse, including biphobic abuse or bullying, it's essential that you reach out for help. There are several amazing organizations listed in this back of this book, including helplines and websites, if you need them.

Another type of biphobia you might experience in a relationship is internalized biphobia. When we enter into a relationship with another person, whether they're the same gender as us or different, it can be easy to let the negative voices creep in that tell you you're not really bi because you've 'picked a side'. Working through this biphobia towards yourself is hard, but completely possible. Your identity isn't defined by your relationship. Whether you're bi and single, bi and monogamous, bi and polyam – you're still bi.

> *I'd advise any young person open to hearing from me that the relationship they have with themselves is the most important one and that working to improve and deepen that relationship will likely mean you're able to show up better in relation to others.* (J.R. YUSSUF (HE/THEY), AUTHOR OF *DEAR BI MEN: A BLACK MAN'S PERSPECTIVE ON POWER, CONSENT, BREAKING DOWN BINARIES, AND COMBATING ERASURE*)

As bi+ people, we have such a great capacity to love beyond limits. Remember to extend that love towards yourself.

Step Bi Step...

- Most of the information we get about dating is focused on two heterosexual people. For bi+ people, this can leave us feeling unprepared if we decide we want to start having romantic relationships.

- Meeting other queer people your age may be challenging but there are plenty of options. Joining an LGBTQIA+ group is a great idea, but you can also (safely) connect with people online.

- There isn't just one relationship style. Monogamy – dating one person at a time – is one option and there are plenty of ways to honour your bi+ identity in a monogamous relationship. Alternatively, some bi+ people have relationships with multiple people (polyamory) because they feel that their bisexuality is erased in monogamous relationships.

- A healthy relationship is one where you feel safe, respected and uplifted by your partner(s), and you make them feel the same way.

- If a partner tries to physically or emotionally hurt you, you might be in an abusive relationship. Bi+ people also sometimes experience biphobic abuse in relationships. If this happens, it's very important that you reach out for help.

Chapter Ten

Sex

When I'm not writing about bisexuality, I'm a sex educator – I go into schools and talk to young people about how to have sex that feels safe, comfortable and enjoyable. Unfortunately, not all sex education is as helpful as it should be. Sometimes, there's a lot of focus on the 'safe' and 'comfortable' parts (which are definitely very, very important) but barely any mention of pleasure or fun. And often, queer sex is forgotten all together. (Are we surprised?)

> *I went to a Church of England school and, after we had some basic sex education, our local vicar came around and explained that sex is for marriage and marriage is between a man and a woman.* (LOIS SHEARING (THEY/SHE/HE), AUTHOR OF *BI THE WAY*, CO-EDITOR OF *IT AIN'T OVER TIL THE BISEXUAL SPEAKS* AND FOUNDER OF THE BI SURVIVORS NETWORK)

This book is all about discovering your sexuality and, for some people, experimenting sexually is a big part of that journey. I want to equip you with some basic information that you'll need if you decide to venture into the world of sexual relationships.

Now, this topic is huge – far bigger than a single chapter can cover. I highly recommend checking out the resources at the back of the book if you still have questions after reading this section.

Also, if you're reading this thinking, 'Whoa, I'm not ready to have sex yet!' – don't worry! This stuff might not even be on your radar yet, and that's fine. But it's never a bad idea to be prepared for all eventualities. You might not use this information for a few years (remember that the age of consent is 16 in the UK, and between 16 and 18 in the USA). You might decide that you never want a sexual relationship. That's completely your choice. But if you find that you do want to explore sex, either now or in the future, at least you'll have the tools you need to make it safe and pleasurable for everyone involved.

What is sex?

You may have been told that sex is when a penis enters a vagina. And while that's true, it's just one of many ways that people might choose to have sex. In reality, sex – like queerness – is very open-ended.

Put simply, sex is about exploring bodies, often in a way that is pleasurable and intimate. If that sounds vague, here's a more technical definition: sex typically involves a person's genitals coming into contact with another person's genitals, anus, mouth, hands, or with sex toys. For example, anal sex is when a penis enters an anus. Oral sex is when one person licks or sucks another person's genitals. And mutual masturbation is when people touch one another's genitals.

But the definition of sex is different for everyone. Some people might count mutual masturbation as sex, while others only consider it to be foreplay (sexual touching in the lead up to sex, like an appetizer before the main meal). Some people consider solo masturbation to be sex, because it involves sexual touching and pleasure, while other people would only consider something to be sex if it involves another person. There's no right or wrong answer – only you get to define what sex looks like for you.

When we only describe sex as a penis going into a vagina, we exclude a lot of queer people for whom this type of sex may never occur. If a woman has never had penis-in-vagina sex, but she has been having oral sex with her wife of 20 years – does that mean she's never had sex?! Of course not.

Sex can be anything you want it to be – but if it does involve someone other than yourself, there are extra steps that you need to take to keep you and your partner(s) safe.

STIs and contraception

Sexually transmitted infections (STIs) are spread through unprotected sexual contact and, when left untreated, they can cause some not-so-fun side effects, from itching and soreness to much more serious problems like infertility.

There are so many myths surrounding STIs – you may have heard some people claim that only people with penises can pass on STIs, and therefore two people with vulvas don't need to use contraception if they're having sex. This is wrong – STIs aren't just transmitted through semen, they can also be passed on through vaginal fluids and skin-to-skin contact.

There's absolutely no shame in getting an STI, but you probably want to avoid them for the sake of your health (just like there's no shame in getting a cold, but you still don't want one!). This is where contraception comes in.

Contraception, also known as birth control, is used to prevent pregnancy, which can occur from penis-in-vagina sex. However, any type of sexual contact with another person – penis-in-vagina sex, anal sex, oral sex, mutual masturbation, genital-to-genital contact and sharing sex toys – can result in the transmission of STIs.

Lots of forms of contraception that are used to prevent pregnancy – like the pill, the implant or the coil – don't stop the transmission of STIs. You'll need what is called a 'barrier method'.

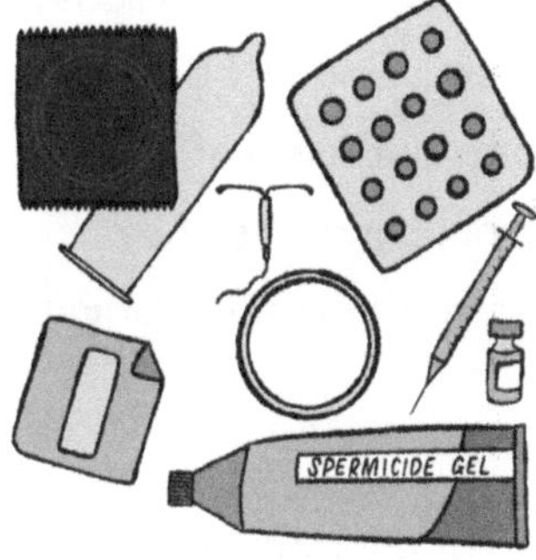

If you're having a type of sex when a penis is entering someone's body (such as a vagina, an anus or a mouth) the barrier method you'd use is a condom. The external condom can be rolled down over an erect penis to stop semen from entering the other person's body. They even come latex-free, for people with latex allergies, and in different flavours for oral sex. (A quick heads-up that flavoured condoms are often coloured to match the flavour. So yes, a mint condom might make a penis look like it belongs to the Incredible Hulk!)

The internal condom is slightly different and is designed to be inserted into the vagina for penis-in-vagina sex. These condoms are not as popular – they can be hard to get hold of. But they're still an option that you have – you may just need to order them online instead of buying them at the corner shop.

'Okay, but what about if I'm giving oral sex to someone with a vulva? How do I protect myself?' Dental dams! Dental dams are sheets of latex that you can stretch over a vulva (or anus) to protect your mouth from STIs and bacteria. Like condoms, they come in a variety of flavours so it doesn't just taste as if you're licking a party balloon.

Unfortunately, there's not a lot of evidence on how effective dental dams are in preventing STI transmission. It's believed that they're less effective than condoms but more effective than using nothing at all. As with internal condoms, they can be hard to find, but you can purchase them online or get them from sexual health clinics.

Sometimes, contraception is forgotten or condoms slip off or break during sex. It happens! This is when you should reach out to a sexual health clinic or your doctor. They'll likely want to give you an STI test and, if you have a uterus, they might prescribe you some emergency contraception to prevent pregnancy. Remember that sexual health professionals aren't there to judge you, they're there to help. And you have a right to confidentiality even if you're under the age of consent.

As a good rule of thumb, you should be getting STI tests every time you change sexual partner, or approximately every six months if you're in a long-term sexual relationship. STI tests are usually free at sexual health clinics, and in certain areas you can even order at-home tests which you can send back in the post. Your results will usually be sent to you by text.

No matter who you're having sex with, or what body parts they have, contraception is a must if you're trying to avoid pregnancy and STIs.

Consent

If contraception is about staying safe physically, then consent is how you ensure that everyone feels safe and comfortable emotionally.

Consent is when you give permission for something to happen – it's a legal requirement when you're engaging in any form of sexual behaviour with another person. Before any type of physical intimacy – from kissing to anal sex – everyone involved needs to agree that they're on board, and happy to proceed. And if someone says no, or they seem uncomfortable, everybody needs to stop immediately.

But there's slightly more to it than this. Let me introduce you to the three pillars of consent: choice, freedom and capacity.

Choice

Choice is what most people think of when they imagine consent – somebody saying, 'Yes, I want to do that' or, 'No, I don't want to do that'. We all have a right to decide whether or not we would like to have sex, and to agree to certain sex acts but not others. For example, you might feel comfortable with mutual masturbation, but say no to oral sex. That's your choice!

But consent isn't quite as simple as hearing a 'yes' and then getting down to business. There are other factors to consider...

Freedom

Okay, so somebody has said 'yes' to sex. They've made the choice. But, in certain circumstances, people may not have the freedom to make that choice. For example, if the person in question is only consenting to sex because they:

- have been pressured or coerced ('I won't believe that you love me unless you have sex with me.')
- are being blackmailed ('If you don't have sex with me I'll post your nudes on Instagram.')
- have been threatened or are at risk of harm ('Have sex with me or I'll hurt you.').

If you're only agreeing to sex because you're scared of what will happen if you say no, that's not consent.

Capacity

Your capacity to consent refers to your ability to fully understand what's going on, and what the potential consequences could be. Certain people are unable to consent to sex, such as those who are:

- under the legal age of consent
- drunk or under the influence of drugs
- asleep, or unconscious.

You might have made a choice, and done so freely. But if you do not also have the capacity to consent, it's not consensual sex.

So, who asks for consent? Our society loves to portray men as always being up for sex, and women as the ones who are less interested (think of every sitcom ever). This can lead to the idea that men have to be the ones to ask for consent, and women have to be the ones to give it.

But this is heteronormative rubbish! Not only do these strict gender roles completely ignore queer relationships and non-binary people, but they're also damaging to straight couples. I'll repeat what I said earlier in this section –

everyone involved needs to agree that they're on board and are happy to proceed. Regardless of gender.

For bi+ folks, this means that the way you ask for and give consent shouldn't change at all depending on the gender of the person you're with. No matter who you're having sex with, you should be checking in with both them and yourself to make sure everyone is happy and having a good time.

Sometimes people worry that asking for consent feels too formal while you're in the throes of passion. But don't worry, you don't need to whip out a pre-prepared contract and get your partner to sign on the dotted line. There are plenty of ways to ask for consent that can be just as sexy as the sex itself:

- 'What do you want me to do to you?'
- 'I want to touch you so badly. Do you want me to touch you?'
- 'Do you like that?'
- 'You look as if you're enjoying that – shall I carry on?'
- 'Would you like more?'

Similarly, you can give consent in equally sexy ways! It can be as simple as saying:

- 'Yes, please do that to me.'

- 'I've actually fantasized about you asking me to do that!'
- 'Mmm, don't stop!'
- 'That feels so good.'
- 'Keep going!'

And while 'no' is a complete sentence and you are well within your right to use it, you might also want to express a desire to slow down or stop in different ways:

- 'Can we pause for a second?'
- 'This isn't working for me. Can we try something else?'
- 'I don't think I'm ready for that yet. Can we just kiss for now?'
- 'I love that you want to do that with me. Let me think about it and maybe next time!'
- 'I thought I'd feel comfortable with this but I actually don't. Can we stop?'

If you have doubts, know that you're always allowed to say no, even if you've done something many times before. Remember that it's normal to feel slightly nervous before you try something new sexually. But it should feel more like excited jitters, rather than actual worry or fear. Sex should be fun, and leave you feeling good both physically and mentally!

Pleasure

Other than to have a baby, one of the main reasons that people have sex is because it has the potential to feel really good. Not only can it cause your body to feel all warm and tingly, but it can also be a wonderful way to connect and have fun with another person.

Lots of people carry shame around pleasure, as if making our bodies feel good in some way makes us bad or dirty. But it's funny how this only really applies to sexual pleasure. There are so many experiences that give us physical pleasure in our daily lives – from sinking into a warm bubble bath, to receiving a deep, invigorating massage, to feeling chocolate melt on our tongue. These sensations aren't necessarily sexual in nature, but they feel pretty pleasurable and we aren't shamed for enjoying them!

You have a body that has the potential to feel really, really good – there's nothing wrong with indulging in that.

> My favourite thing about being bisexual is the bi+, sex-positive, polyamorous community. I have found my PEOPLE living in Brooklyn. And these folks make me feel accepted, supported and loved for who I am.
> (ZACHARY ZANE (HE/HIM), COLUMNIST AND AUTHOR)

Queer people in particular may feel even more shame for enjoying sex. Sadly, this is because, while sex is considered a social taboo, being queer is an even bigger one. We might feel that we're doing something sinful or wrong when we have sex – something that doesn't fit the only socially acceptable script: 'cisgender man puts penis in cisgender woman's vagina'.

For bi+ people who are repeatedly told that they're sex-crazed animals who'll hook up with anything that moves, relaxing and welcoming pleasure into our lives can feel as if we're proving the haters right – that we, somehow, are affirming harmful biphobic stereotypes.

I know I've had this fear. But in reality, there's nothing wrong with enjoying sex. No matter what type of sex you're having, or with however many people, as long as everyone involved has given consent you have no reason to be ashamed.

Masturbation

Masturbation, or solo sex, can be a great way to explore your own fantasies and boundaries safely. It can help you to figure out how you like to be touched so that you can communicate this with current or future partners, but it can also give you space to explore your sexuality solo, before you involve other people.

> *I wasn't sexually active until my twenties, so my desires remained ambiguous and amorphous for a while. It's a much more generous place to discover and decide who you are – as well as leaving room for who you might become.* (DESIREE BURCH (SHE/HER), COMEDIAN AND PERFORMANCE ARTIST)

There's a lot of negative myths surrounding masturbation (when I was a teenager, I heard it makes you go blind!) but they're not true. When done safely, masturbation can actually *benefit* your health, reducing stress, helping you sleep, improving your mood and even easing menstrual cramps. (All the perks of exercise but lying down!)

Of course, there's absolutely no pressure to masturbate.

Some people just don't want to and that's absolutely fine. But if you have a desire to masturbate, or you masturbate already, it's important that you know there's nothing wrong with you and you're not going to go blind, get hairy palms or any other urban myth about self-pleasure that has been proven wrong again and again!

Different strokes for different folks

I've encountered many bi+ people who are nervous about having sex with someone who has genitals they're not used to. For example, if you've only ever had sex with someone with a penis, how on earth are you supposed to know what to do with a vulva?! It can feel as if you've learned how to drive a car and now you're supposed to operate a motorbike.

But here's the thing. Every set of genitals is different. No two penises are identical and neither are two vulvas. Each time you get intimate with somebody new, it's a brand-new playing field. You should approach every person's body as a blank slate of possibilities and pleasure, even if they have the same kind of genitals as your last partner.

What works for one person's vulva won't necessarily work for another person's. That thing that your ex-boyfriend *loved*? Your new boyfriend might hate it! I remember growing up and thinking that one day I would master the art of sex. But in reality, getting really good at sex with one person doesn't mean that you'll be equally skilled with the next person you sleep with. With every new partner, it takes time to discover their likes and dislikes, their boundaries and your rhythm as a couple.

There's also a common misconception that it's easier to have sex with someone who has the same type of genitals as you because you already know what feels good, and you've had the chance to practise on your own body. But again, what works for you personally won't necessarily ignite the same sparks in your partner.

Sex is about discovery, playfulness and curiosity. It's about approaching bodies (including your own) with an open mind. If something doesn't work, it's about laughing it off and moving on to the next thing. Queer sex is liberating because it already diverts from society's script – it bursts our possibilities wide open.

Porn would have you think that sex should be a well-rehearsed play, a line never missed and a prop never dropped. But really, sex is improv – sharing the stage with people you trust, a vague sense of where you want to go but the openness to explore, play and adapt, and the power to call 'scene' whenever it feels right.

Step Bi Step...

- Queer sex might look different from the most common depiction of sex – penis-in-vagina – and that's fine. Only you get to define what sex means to you.

- Using contraception is important during any type of sex with another person as it protects you from STIs and, in the case of penis-in-vagina sex, unwanted pregnancy.

- Consent is essential, no matter what type of sex you're having, or with who. Everyone involved must be given a choice, and have the freedom and capacity to make that choice.

- Pleasure isn't shameful. You are allowed to enjoy giving and receiving pleasure. You should approach every new partner with an open mind, as no two bodies are the same. Sex should be playful, exploratory and fun.

Epilogue

We started this book with my own bi journey – I'd like to end it with yours.

There is a lot I cannot tell you. I can't tell you at what age you'll feel as if you've 'figured out' your identity. I don't know if 'bisexual' or 'pansexual' or 'queer' are the right labels for you. I can't decide when you'll come out to your friends and family, and I have no way of knowing how people will respond to your queerness, or how easy a ride you will have. These steps, with their triumphs and challenges, are yours to take. But what I do know is this:

You will find your people. There is an enormous community of bi+ people out there, ready to welcome you with open arms. Whether you party at Bi Pride every year, or simply find a few select bi+ friends that you can really trust, you will discover the joy of sharing your queerness with other people. You will, at some point in your life, feel that you are part of something bigger than yourself.

You will carve your own path. For many of us, our teen years are spent trying to find out where we fit in. But inevitably, you will come to realize (if you haven't already) that fitting in is overrated and that it's far more fun to craft a life that feels original and authentic to you. You will embrace your queerness no matter how unconventional it feels, and define your identity on your own terms. And with that, you'll feel a sense of liberation unlike any other.

You will see things change. The world and its attitudes to bi+ people are constantly evolving. When I began school in the early 2000s, it was illegal for teachers to even mention gay and bi identities. Now, two decades later, I teach in schools where Pride flags adorn the hallways. You will see the world become a more accepting place for bi+ people, and feel optimistic for the generations that come after you. And, I hope, you will play a part in making that change.

You will become stronger. Being a bi+ person can come with challenges, but in time, you will grow more and more confident in using your voice – in standing up for yourself and your community. You'll one day feel able to disregard the opinions of people who want you to exist in greyscale, and fight back by flourishing in full colour.

You will love yourself. I hope you already do. But if you don't yet, you will. You will come to recognize that there will only ever be one of you, and that it would be a catastrophic shame to fail to appreciate this once-in-a-universe individual. You will feel proud of yourself, and you'll cherish every quirk and every difference that sets you apart from the crowd.

The journey will be long, and may continue well into adulthood – I myself am still learning what my identity means to me, and have to remind myself to practise the self-compassion that I preach to others.

I hope, however, that this book has helped you on your way, that you feel you can come back to it if you want a reminder of your worth, or as you encounter new challenges in your life. I hope it acts as a friend – providing you with reassurance and advice, whenever you need it.

But now, I must pass it over to you – you've got this.

Further Support

If you're in need of further support or information, the following services are there to help you. Some have helplines you can call, others have useful information on their websites. Never be afraid to reach out.

The services marked with ✿ are LGBTQIA+-specific, while the ones without cater to everyone.

Gender and sexuality

Switchboard✿
A UK LGBTQIA+ support line.
Helpline: 0800 0119 100
Website: www.switchboard.lgbt

LGBT National Help Center✿
A USA non-profit supporting LGBTQIA+ young people and adults.
Helpline: 800 246 7743
Website: www.lgbthotline.org

Just Like Us✿
A UK LGBT+ young people's charity.
Website: www.justlikeus.org

Mermaids[✿]
A UK charity for trans, non-binary and gender-diverse young people.
Helpline: 0808 801 0400
Website: www.mermaidsuk.org.uk

Mental health and wellbeing

Childline
A UK-based helpline for children and young people.
Helpline: 0800 1111
Website: www.childline.org.uk

Rainbow Mind[✿]
A charity supporting LGBTQIA+ people with mental health issues in the UK.
Website: www.rainbowmind.org

PAPYRUS
A UK young people's charity dedicated to the prevention of suicide.
Helpline: 0800 068 41 41
Website: www.papyrus-uk.org

The Trevor Project[✿]
A USA organization focusing on suicide prevention in LGBTQ+ youth.
Helpline: 1 866 488 7386
Website: www.thetrevorproject.org

Abuse and violence

Galop✿
A UK charity for LGBT+ survivors of abuse, violence and hate crime.
Helpline: 0800 999 5428
Website: www.galop.org.uk

Bi Survivors Network✿
Peer-led, online support groups for bi+ survivors of sexual and/or domestic violence.
Website: www.bisurvivorsnetwork.org

Zero Abuse Project
An organization working with young survivors of sexual abuse in the USA.
Helpline: 800-325-HOPE
Website: www.zeroabuseproject.org

Sex and relationships

Brook
A sexual health charity for young people in the UK.
Website: www.brook.org.uk

Planned Parenthood
A USA organization providing sexual health and abortion care.
Helpline: 1 800 230 PLAN
Website: www.plannedparenthood.org

Fumble
A free digital sex education resource for young people.
Website: www.fumble.org.uk

Housing

AKT

A UK LGBTQIA+ youth homelessness charity.
Website: www.akt.org.uk

Stonewall Housing

A charity supporting LGBTQIA+ people of all ages in the UK who are experiencing homelessness or living in an unsafe environment.
Website: www.stonewallhousing.org

True Colours United

A charity supporting homeless LGBTQ+ young people in the USA.
Website: www.truecolorsunited.org

Acknowledgements

This book wouldn't have been possible without the input of so many fantastic people – from bi+ trailblazers to those who have surrounded me with love and support. I would like to take this opportunity to extend my most sincere and heartfelt thanks.

First, to you, the reader, for picking up this little book and trusting me with such an important piece of yourself.

To Lewis, Mark, AFLO and Eliza, for adding dimensions that I never could, and to every other bi+ person who shared their stories, advice and insights. The queer community is all the more powerful with you in it.

To Dr Caitriona Cox, Cody Daigle-Orians, Tash Oakes-Monger, Leanne Yau and Kimberly Zieselman, for checking parts of the text for accuracy and sensitivity. You have made this book stronger than I ever could have alone.

To Jane and the whole team at JKP, for giving me this opportunity and, in doing so, fulfilling my lifelong dream of becoming an author.

To Laura (the other one!), for lending your immense talent to this book in the form of such beautiful illustrations. And for being the most supportive, wonderful friend.

To my girl gang – Rhian, Kudzai, Charlie, Petra, Beth and Becca – for embracing my many quirks ever since we were teenagers. I love you guys.

To Libby, for being my best friend. For holding me while I cried in a hotel room in Leeds, and telling me to quit my job and 'go write a book'. This, and so much of who I am, is because of you.

To my parents, for a lifetime of support. Thank you for nurturing my love of reading as a child – for the weekly trips to Dolphin Books and for telling me, and everyone else, that I would be an author someday. You made me believe it.

And finally, to Conor, for literally everything – from your scrupulous proofreading, to your endless love and encouragement. You are undoubtedly my biggest and most unwavering ally.

Endnotes

Chapter One

1. Nagoski, E. (2024) *Come Together: The Science (and Art) of Creating Lasting Sexual Connections*. London: Vermilion.
2. Faye, S. (2021) *The Transgender Issue: An Argument for Justice*. Bristol: Allen Lane.

Chapter Two

1. Ochs, R. (2024) Get to know Robyn Ochs [Internet]. Robyn Ochs. Available from: www.robynochs.com.

Chapter Three

1. Cantarella, E. (2002) *Bisexuality in the Ancient World*. New Haven: Yale Nota Bene.
2. Berg, A. (2020) The evolution of the word 'bisexual' – and why it's still misunderstood [Internet]. NBC News. Available from: www.nbcnews.com/feature/nbc-out/evolution-word-bisexual-why-it-s-still-misunderstood-n1240832
3. Jones, J. (2024) LGBTQ+ identification in U.S. now at 7.6% [Internet]. Gallup. Available from: https://news.gallup.com/poll/611864/lgbtq-identification.aspx
4. Office for National Statistics. (2023) Sexual orientation, UK: 2021

and 2022 [Internet]. www.ons.gov.uk. Available from: www.ons.gov.uk/peoplepopulationandcommunity/culturalidentity/sexuality/bulletins/sexualidentityuk/2021and2022

5. Office for National Statistics. (2023) Sexual orientation, UK: 2021 and 2022 [Internet]. www.ons.gov.uk. Available from: www.ons.gov.uk/peoplepopulationandcommunity/culturalidentity/sexuality/bulletins/sexualidentityuk/2021and2022
6. The Bay Area Bisexual Network. (1990) Beyond the Myths of Bisexuality. Anything That Moves, 1.
7. Bisexuality. In: Cambridge Dictionary [Internet]. Available from: https://dictionary.cambridge.org/dictionary/english/bisexuality
8. Stonewall. List of LGBTQ+ terms [Internet]. Stonewall. Available from: www.stonewall.org.uk/resources/list-lgbtq-terms?
9. Birner, B. (2002) Bilingualism [Internet]. Washington, DC: Linguistic Society of America. Available from: https://old.linguisticsociety.org/sites/default/files/Bilingual.pdf
10. Shearing, L. (2021) *Bi the Way*. London: Jessica Kingsley Publishers.
11. Spalding, L.R. & Peplau, L.A. (1997) The unfaithful lover. *Psychology of Women Quarterly*, 21(4):611–625.
12. Mehta, V. (2022) Bi+ visibility, the AIDS crisis, & the demonisation of bisexual men [Internet]. Rainbow & Co. Available from: https://rainbowandco.uk/blogs/what-were-saying/bi-visibility-2022
13. Everett, B.G., Schnarrs, P.W., Rosario, M., Garofalo, R. & Mustanski, B. (2014) Sexual orientation disparities in sexually transmitted infection risk behaviors and risk determinants among sexually active adolescent males: Results from a school-based sample. *American Journal of Public Health*, 104(6):1107–1112.
14. Phallocentrism. In: Cambridge Dictionary [Internet]. Available from: https://dictionary.cambridge.org/dictionary/english/phallocentrism
15. Compton, J. (2017) #StillBisexual campaign founder fights for bi-visibility [Internet]. NBC News. Available from: www.nbcnews.com/

feature/nbc-out/outfront-stillbisexual-campaign-founder-fights-bi-visibility-n721736

Chapter Four

1. Rapoport, E. (2009) Bisexuality in psychoanalytic theory: Interpreting the resistance. *Journal of Bisexuality*, 9(3–4): 279–295.

2. Shearing, L. (2023) If bisexuality was a choice, I'd choose it any day [Internet]. Cosmopolitan. Available from: www.cosmopolitan.com/uk/love-sex/relationships/a45265950/bisexuality-isnt-a-choice

3. Shearing, L. (2021) *Bi the Way*. London: Jessica Kingsley Publishers.

4. Diamond, L.M. (2008) Female bisexuality from adolescence to adulthood: Results from a 10-year longitudinal study. *Developmental Psychology*, 44(1):5–14.

5. #StillBisexual. About us [Internet]. #StillBisexual. Available from: https://stillbi.org/about-us

6. #StillBisexual. About us [Internet]. #StillBisexual. Available from: https://stillbi.org/about-us

7. Puckett, L. (2017) 9 bisexual women who are making History [Internet]. Teen Vogue. Available from: www.teenvogue.com/gallery/bisexual-women-making-history

8. Rapp, R. (2024) If I say I'm a lesbian I am a lesbian and if someone says they're bi they are bi. I've had enough of you witches [X post]. Available from: https://x.com/reneerapp/status/1772328346917159164

Chapter Five

1. Jones, J. (2024) LGBTQ+ identification in U.S. now at 7.6% [Internet]. Gallup. Available from: https://news.gallup.com/poll/611864/lgbtq-identification.aspx

2. Thames TV. (1979) David Bowie interview. Afternoon plus [Internet]. YouTube. 2016. Available from: www.youtube.com/watch?v=LwTFW4kfHl4

3. Chudy, E. (2022) Kristen Stewart says her sexuality is 'confusing for other people' but refuses to 'hide anything' [Internet]. PinkNews. Available from: www.thepinknews.com/2022/03/28/kristen-stewart-sexuality-coming-out-bisexual

4. Brammer, J.P. (2018) There's hope for a Freddie Mercury biopic without straight-washing [Internet]. them. Available from: www.them.us/story/theres-hope-for-a-freddie-mercury-biopic-without-straight-washing

5. GLAAD. (2024) Where we are on TV [Internet]. GLAAD. Available from: https://assets.glaad.org/m/7c489f209e120a11/original/GLAAD-2023-24-Where-We-Are-on-TV.pdf

6. Jones, J. (2024) LGBTQ+ identification in U.S. now at 7.6% [Internet]. Gallup. Available from: https://news.gallup.com/poll/611864/lgbtq-identification.aspx

7. Milward, C. (2019) 13 times soaps broke LGBTQ+ ground on TV [Internet]. Digital Spy. Available from: www.digitalspy.com/soaps/eastenders/a860766/times-soaps-broke-lgbtq-ground

8. Galton, S. (2020) Natalie Cassidy laughs through kissing girls – and says she gets less stubble rash [Internet]. The Mirror. Available from: www.mirror.co.uk/3am/celebrity-news/natalie-cassidy-laughs-through-kissing-21467203

9. Houghton, R. (2022) EastEnders star Natalie Cassidy addresses Sonia Fowler's sexuality [Internet]. Digital Spy. Available from: www.digitalspy.com/soaps/eastenders/a40385752/eastenders-sonia-fowler-sexuality-natalie-cassidy/#r3z-addoor

10. Eastenders Banter. (2022) Part time lesbian, full time nurse and mum to Bex – Sonia has got quite the flex! From hero to zero – saving Ben with a pen to robbing poor Dot, a part time lesbian with a conscience – I think not!!! #moderndayshakespeare 25 April [Facebook post]. Available from: www.facebook.com/eastendersbanter16/posts/part-

time-lesbian-full-time-nurse-and-mum-to-bex-sonia-has-got-quite-the-flex-fr/3117722728489252

11. Shearing, L. (2019) Introducing the Ramirez Test [Internet]. Medium. Available from: https://medium.com/@lois.shearing/introducing-the-ramirez-test-b91e98b57d1d

12. Shearing, L. (2019) Introducing the Ramirez Test [Internet]. Medium. Available from: https://medium.com/@lois.shearing/introducing-the-ramirez-test-b91e98b57d1d

13. Kilkelly, D. (2017) BBC Drama boss Oliver Kent wants better bisexual representation in EastEnders, Casualty and Holby City [Internet]. Digital Spy. Available from: www.digitalspy.com/soaps/eastenders/a833027/oliver-kent-bisexual-storylines-eastenders-casualty-holby

14. Kilkelly, D. (2017) BBC Drama boss Oliver Kent wants better bisexual representation in EastEnders, Casualty and Holby City [Internet]. Digital Spy. Available from: www.digitalspy.com/soaps/eastenders/a833027/oliver-kent-bisexual-storylines-eastenders-casualty-holby

Chapter Six

1. Wakefield, L. & Kelleher, P. (2022) The terrible, brutal history of Margaret Thatcher's homophobic Section 28 [Internet]. PinkNews. Available from: www.thepinknews.com/2022/11/18/what-was-section-28-law-lgbt

2. LGBT+marketing. (2013) Margaret Thatcher's anti-gay speech (1:00 min) [Internet]. YouTube. Available from: www.youtube.com/watch?v=8VRRWuryb4k

3. Bradlow, J., Bartram, F., Guasp, A. & Jadva, V. (2017) *School Report: The Experiences of Lesbian, Gay, Bi and Trans Young People in Britain's Schools in 2017* [Internet]. Stonewall. Available from: https://files.stonewall.org.uk/production/files /the_school_report_2017.pdf?dm=1724230520

4. Bradlow, J., Bartram, F., Guasp, A. & Jadva, V. (2017) *School Report: The Experiences of Lesbian, Gay, Bi and Trans Young People in Britain's*

Schools in 2017 [Internet]. Stonewall. Available from: https://files.stonewall.org.uk/production/files /the_school_report_2017.pdf?dm=1724230520

5. Melville, S. & Stonborough, E. (2020) *LGBT in Britain: Bi Report* [Internet]. Stonewall. Available from: https://files.stonewall.org.uk/production/files/lgbt_in_britain_bi.pdf?dm=1724230505
6. Melville, S. & Stonborough, E. (2020) *LGBT in Britain: Bi Report* [Internet]. Stonewall. Available from: https://files.stonewall.org.uk/production/files/lgbt_in_britain_bi.pdf?dm=1724230505
7. York, T. (2021) People erase my existence [Internet]. The British Psychological Society. Available from: www.bps.org.uk/psychologist/people-erase-my-existence
8. Burston, P. (2012) Bisexuality in the workplace: LGBT networks aren't enough [Internet]. The Guardian. Available from: www.theguardian.com/careers/bisexuality-in-workplace-lgbt-networks
9. Bachmann, C.L. & Gooch, B. (2018) *LGBT in Britain: Work Report* [Internet]. Stonewall. Available from: https://files.stonewall.org.uk/production/files/lgbt_in_britain_work_report.pdf?dm=1724230506
10. Melville, S. & Stonborough, E. (2020) *LGBT in Britain: Bi Report* [Internet]. Stonewall. Available from: https://files.stonewall.org.uk/production/files/lgbt_in_britain_bi.pdf?dm=1724230505
11. Nelson, R. & Clarke, L. (2024) *Hard Done Bi: An Exploration of Bi+ Health Inequalities in England* [Internet]. The National LGBT Partnership. Available from: www.consortium.lgbt/wp-content/uploads/2024/03/Hard-Done-Bi-2024.pdf
12. Nelson, R. & Clarke, L. (2024) *Hard Done Bi: An Exploration of Bi+ Health Inequalities in England* [Internet]. The National LGBT Partnership. Available from: www.consortium.lgbt/wp-content/uploads/2024/03/Hard-Done-Bi-2024.pdf
13. Melville, S. & Stonborough, E. (2020) *LGBT in Britain: Bi Report* [Internet]. Stonewall. Available from: https://files.stonewall.org.uk/production/files/lgbt_in_britain_bi.pdf?dm=1724230505

14. Nelson, R. & Clarke, L. (2024) *Hard Done Bi: An Exploration of Bi+ Health Inequalities in England* [Internet]. The National LGBT Partnership. Available from: www.consortium.lgbt/wp-content/uploads/2024/03/Hard-Done-Bi-2024.pdf

15. Nelson, R. & Clarke, L. (2024) *Hard Done Bi: An Exploration of Bi+ Health Inequalities in England* [Internet]. The National LGBT Partnership. Available from: www.consortium.lgbt/wp-content/uploads/2024/03/Hard-Done-Bi-2024.pdf

16. Nelson, R. & Clarke, L. (2024) *Hard Done Bi: An Exploration of Bi+ Health Inequalities in England* [Internet]. The National LGBT Partnership. Available from: www.consortium.lgbt/wp-content/uploads/2024/03/Hard-Done-Bi-2024.pdf

17. Hong, C., Feinstein, B.A., Holloway, I.W., Yu, F. *et al.* (2022) Differences in sexual behaviors, HIV testing, and willingness to use PrEP between gay and bisexual men who have sex with men in China. *International Journal of Sexual Health*, 34(3):424–431.

18. Nelson, R. & Clarke, L. (2024) *Hard Done Bi: An Exploration of Bi+ Health Inequalities in England* [Internet]. The National LGBT Partnership. Available from: www.consortium.lgbt/wp-content/uploads/2024/03/Hard-Done-Bi-2024.pdf

19. Nelson, R. & Clarke, L. (2024) *Hard Done Bi: An Exploration of Bi+ Health Inequalities in England* [Internet]. The National LGBT Partnership. Available from: www.consortium.lgbt/wp-content/uploads/2024/03/Hard-Done-Bi-2024.pdf

20. Powys, M.E. (2020) Bisexual man ordered to pay ex-wife thousands after she accused him of hiding his homosexuality. Only, he's not gay [Internet]. PinkNews. Available from: www.thepinknews.com/2020/12/08/javier-vilalta-bisexual-man-ex-wife-lawsuit-hide-homosexuality-court-order-compensation

21. Powys, M.E. (2021) Judge overturns absurd ruling that forced bi man to pay ex-wife thousands for 'hiding sexuality' [Internet]. PinkNews. Available from: www.thepinknews.com/2021/08/03/javier-vilalta-bisexual-lawsuit-ex-wife-spain

22. Shearing, L. (2021) *Bi the Way*. London: Jessica Kingsley Publishers.

23. Melville, S. & Stonborough, E. (2020) *LGBT in Britain: Bi Report* [Internet]. Stonewall. Available from: https://files.stonewall.org.uk/production/files/lgbt_in_britain_bi.pdf?dm=1724230505

24. McLean, K. (2008) Inside, outside, nowhere: Bisexual men and women in the gay and lesbian community. *Journal of Bisexuality*, 8(1–2):63–80.

25. McLean, K. (2008) Inside, outside, nowhere: Bisexual men and women in the gay and lesbian community. *Journal of Bisexuality*, 8(1–2):63–80.

26. Goodman, E. (2019) Meet 'The Mother of Pride,' the pioneering bisexual activist Brenda Howard [Internet]. them. Available from: www.them.us/story/brenda-howard

27. Melville, S. & Stonborough, E. (2020) *LGBT in Britain: Bi Report* [Internet]. Stonewall. Available from: https://files.stonewall.org.uk/production/files/lgbt_in_britain_bi.pdf?dm=1724230505

28. Nelson, R. & Clarke, L. (2024) *Hard Done Bi: An Exploration of Bi+ Health Inequalities in England* [Internet]. The National LGBT Partnership. Available from: www.consortium.lgbt/wp-content/uploads/2024/03/Hard-Done-Bi-2024.pdf

29. Office for National Statistics. (2022) UK health indicators: 2019 to 2020 [Internet]. www.ons.gov.uk. Available from: www.ons.gov.uk/peoplepopulationandcommunity/healthandsocialcare/healthandlifeexpectancies/bulletins/ukhealthindicators/2019to2020

30. Nelson, R. & Clarke, L. (2024) *Hard Done Bi: An Exploration of Bi+ Health Inequalities in England* [Internet]. The National LGBT Partnership. Available from: www.consortium.lgbt/wp-content/uploads/2024/03/Hard-Done-Bi-2024.pdf

31. Melville, S. & Stonborough, E. (2020) *LGBT in Britain: Bi Report* [Internet]. Stonewall. Available from: https://files.stonewall.org.uk/production/files/lgbt_in_britain_bi.pdf?dm=1724230505

32. Browne, K. & Law, A. (2007) *Count Me In Too: Initial Findings LGBT Community Report* [Internet]. University of Brighton. Available from: https://bpb-eu-w2.wpmucdn.com/blogs.brighton.ac.uk/dist/2/6377/files/2019/12/CMIT_InitialFindings_LGBTCommunityReport_June07.pdf

33. King, M. & McKeown, E. (2003) *Mental Health and Social Wellbeing of Gay Men, Lesbians and Bisexuals in England and Wales* [Internet]. London: Mind. Available from: https://mindout.org.uk/wp-content/uploads/2012/06/SummaryfindingsofLGBreport.pdf

34. Saunders, C.L., Massou, E., Waller, J., Meads, C., Marlow, L.A. & Usher-Smith, J.A. (2021) Cervical screening attendance and cervical cancer risk among women who have sex with women. *Journal of Medical Screening*, 28(3):096914132098727.

Chapter Seven

1. Crenshaw, K. (1989) Demarginalizing the intersection of race and sex: A Black feminist critique of antidiscrimination doctrine, feminist theory and antiracist politics. University of Chicago Legal Forum [Internet]. Available from: https://chicagounbound.uchicago.edu/cgi/viewcontent.cgi?article=1052&context=uclf

2. London bus attack: Boys told couple 'to show how lesbians have sex.' (2019) [Internet]. BBC News. Available from: www.bbc.co.uk/news/uk-england-london-50600887

3. Hannigan, C. (2019) You saw me covered in blood on a bus. But do you get outraged about all homophobia? [Internet]. The Guardian. Available from: www.theguardian.com/commentisfree/2019/jun/14/homophobic-attack-bus-outrage-media-white

4. Eisner, S. (2013) *Bi: Notes for a Bisexual Revolution*. Berkeley, CA: Seal Press.

5. Mulvey, L. (1975) *Visual Pleasure and Narrative Cinema*. London Afterall Books.

6. Walters, M., Chen, J. & Breiding, M. (2013) *The National Intimate Partner and Sexual Violence Survey: 2010 Findings on Victimization by Sexual Orientation*. Atlanta, GA: National Center for Injury Prevention and Control, Centers for Disease Control and Prevention.

7. Walters, M., Chen, J. & Breiding, M. (2013) *The National Intimate Partner and Sexual Violence Survey: 2010 Findings on Victimization by Sexual Orientation*. Atlanta, GA: National Center for Injury Prevention and Control, Centers for Disease Control and Prevention.

8. Wilson, B.D.M., Bouton, L.J.A., Badgett, M.V.L. & Macklin, M.L. (2023) *LGBT Poverty in the United States: Trends at the Onset of COVID-19* [Internet]. UCLA School of Law Williams Institute. Available from: https://williamsinstitute.law.ucla.edu/wp-content/uploads/LGBT-Poverty-COVID-Feb-2023.pdf

9. Green, K.E. & Feinstein, B.A. (2012) Substance use in lesbian, gay, and bisexual populations: An update on empirical research and implications for treatment. *Psychology of Addictive Behaviors*, 26(2):265–278. Available from: www.ncbi.nlm.nih.gov/pmc/articles/PMC3288601

10. Colledge, L., Hickson, F., Reid, D. & Weatherburn, P. (2015) Poorer mental health in UK bisexual women than lesbians: Evidence from the UK 2007 Stonewall Women's Health Survey. *Journal of Public Health*, 37(3):427–437.

11. Melville, S. & Stonborough, E. (2020) *LGBT in Britain: Bi Report* [Internet]. Stonewall. Available from: https://files.stonewall.org.uk/production/files/lgbt_in_britain_bi.pdf?dm=1724230505

12. Hartman, J. (2006) Another kind of 'chilly climate.' *Journal of Bisexuality*, 5(4):61–76.

13. Vrangalova, Z. (2018) A new study explains why many lesbians are biased against bisexual women [Internet] them. Available from: www.them.us/story/study-explains-lesbian-bias-against-bisexual-women

14. Tsoulis-Reay, A. (2016) Are you straight, gay, or just...you? [Internet]. Glamour. Available from: www.glamour.com/story/glamour-sexuality-survey

15. Ballard, J. (2019) Millennials are more open to a bisexual partner than older generations – but not by much. YouGov.

16. Gleason, N., Vencill, J.A. & Sprankle, E. (2018) Swipe left on the bi guys: Examining attitudes toward dating and being sexual with bisexual individuals. *Journal of Bisexuality*, 18(4):516–534.

17. Melville, S. & Stonborough, E. (2020) *LGBT in Britain: Bi Report* [Internet]. Stonewall. Available from: https://files.stonewall.org.uk/production/files/lgbt_in_britain_bi.pdf?dm=1724230505

18. Pew Research Center. (2013) *A Survey of LGBT Americans Attitudes, Experiences and Values in Changing Times* [Internet]. Pew Research Center. Available from: www.pewresearch.org/wp-content/uploads/sites/20/2013/06/SDT_LGBT-Americans_06-2013.pdf

19. Schin, A. (2023) Not all unicorns and rainbows [Internet]. Taimi. Available from: https://taimi.com/news/not-all-unicorns-and-rainbows

20. Reisner, S.L., Choi, S.K., Herman, J.L., Bockting, W., Krueger, E.A. & Meyer, I.H. (2023) Sexual Orientation in Transgender Adults in the United States. *BMC Public Health*, 23(1):1799.

21. White, N. (2024) What is 'Global Majority' and why is it replacing 'BAME'? [Internet]. The Independent. Available from: www.independent.co.uk/news/uk/home-news/global-majority-bame-explained-national-trust-b2546898.html

22. Han, E. & O'Mahoney, J. (2014) British Colonialism and the criminalization of homosexuality. *Cambridge Review of International Affairs*, 27(2):268–288.

23. Han, E. & O'Mahoney, J. (2014) British Colonialism and the criminalization of homosexuality. *Cambridge Review of International Affairs*, 27(2):268–288.

24. Han, E. & O'Mahoney, J. (2014) British Colonialism and the criminalization of homosexuality. *Cambridge Review of International Affairs*, 27(2):268–288.

25. Roscoe, W. (1996) *The Zuni Man-Woman.* Albuquerque: University of New Mexico Press.

26. Brown, L. (2014) *Two Spirit People: American Indian Lesbian Women and Gay Men.* London: Routledge.

27. Roscoe, W. (1996) *The Zuni Man-Woman.* Albuquerque, NM: University of New Mexico Press.

28. Nanda, S. (1990) *Neither Man Nor Woman.* Belmont, CA: Wadsworth Publishing.

29. Nanda, S. (1990) *Neither Man Nor Woman.* Belmont, CA: Wadsworth Publishing.

30. Nanda, S. (1990) *Neither Man Nor Woman.* Belmont, CA: Wadsworth Publishing.

31. Horswell, M.J. (2003) Toward an Andean Theory of Ritual, Same-Sex Sexuality and Third-Gender Subjectivity. In: P. Sigal (ed.) *Infamous Desire* (pp.25–69). Chicago, IL: University of Chicago Press.

32. Horswell, M.J. (2003) Toward an Andean Theory of Ritual, Same-Sex Sexuality and Third-Gender Subjectivity. In: P. Sigal (ed.) *Infamous Desire* (pp.25–69). Chicago, IL: University of Chicago Press.

33. Aspin, C. & Hutchings, J. (2007) Reclaiming the past to inform the future: Contemporary views of Maori sexuality. *Culture, Health & Sexuality*, 9(4):415–427.

34. Aspin, C. & Hutchings, J. (2007) Reclaiming the past to inform the future: Contemporary views of Maori sexuality. *Culture, Health & Sexuality*, 9(4):415–427.

35. Olupona, J.K. (1991) *African Traditional Religions in Contemporary Society.* Westport, CT: Greenwood Press.

36. Ako, E. Y. (2023) Same-sex relationships and recriminalisation of homosexuality in Ghana. *Sociolinguistic Studies*, 17(1–3):45–65.

37. Ako, E. Y. (2023) Same-sex relationships and recriminalisation of homosexuality in Ghana. *Sociolinguistic Studies*, 17(1–3):45–65.

38. Conner, R. (2003) Sexuality and Gender in African Spiritual Traditions. In: D.W. Machacek & M.M. Wilcox (eds) *Sexuality and the World's Religions* (pp.3–30). London: Bloomsbury Publishing.

39. Conner, R. (2003) Sexuality and Gender in African Spiritual Traditions. In: D.W. Machacek & M.M. Wilcox (eds) *Sexuality and the World's Religions* (pp.3–30). Londoun: Bloomsbury Publishing.

40. Griaule, M. (1965) *Conversations with Ogotemmêli: An Introduction to Dogon Religious Ideas.* Oxford: Oxford University Press.

41. Nyanzi, S. (2013) Dismantling reified African culture through localised homosexualities in Uganda. *Culture, Health & Sexuality*, 15(8):952–967.

42. Melville, S. & Stonborough, E. (2020) *LGBT in Britain: Bi Report* [Internet]. Stonewall. Available from: https://files.stonewall.org.uk/production/files/lgbt_in_britain_bi.pdf?dm=1724230505

43. ParaPride. (2024) About [Internet]. ParaPride. Available from: www.parapride.org/about

Dear Reader,

We'd love your attention for one more page to tell you about the crisis in children's reading, and what we can all do.

Studies have shown that reading for fun is the **single biggest predictor of a child's future life chances** – more than family circumstance, parents' educational background or income. It improves academic results, mental health, wealth, communication skills, ambition and happiness.[1]

The number of children reading for fun is in rapid decline. Young people have a lot of competition for their time. In 2024, 1 in 10 children and young people in the UK aged 5 to 18 did not own a single book at home.[2]

Hachette works extensively with schools, libraries and literacy charities, but here are some ways we can all raise more readers:

- Reading to children for just 10 minutes a day makes a difference
- Don't give up if children aren't regular readers – there will be books for them!
- Visit bookshops and libraries to get recommendations
- Encourage them to listen to audiobooks
- Support school libraries
- Give books as gifts

There's a lot more information about how to encourage children to read on our website: **www.RaisingReaders.co.uk**

Thank you for reading.

hachette UK

---

1 National Literacy Trust, 'Book Ownership in 2024', November 2024, https://literacytrust.org.uk/research-services/research-reports/book-ownership-in-2024

2 OECD, '21st-Century Readers: Developing Literacy Skills in a Digital World', OECD Publishing, Paris, 2021, https://www.oecd.org/en/publications/21st-century-readers_a83d84cb-en.html